57

BY THE SAME AUTHOR

THE USE OF WORDS

    BOOK ONE: FOR JUNIOR FORMS

    BOOK TWO: FOR THE MIDDLE SCHOOL

    BOOK THREE: ENGLISH—A G.C.E. COURSE

THE COMMAND
OF ENGLISH

A Certificate Course for Practical People

T. H. HEWSON, M.A.

★

LONDON
JOHN MURRAY, ALBEMARLE STREET, W.

First published 1955
Reprinted 1957
Reprinted 1959
Reprinted 1961
Reprinted 1964

Made and Printed in Great Britain by C. Tinling & Co., Ltd.,
Liverpool, London and Prescot, and published by John Murray (Publishers) Ltd.

FOREWORD

THIS book is intended as a text-book for the various Certificate examinations taken in Technical Colleges and Schools. It is an adaptation of my book *English : A General Certificate Course* which a number of Technical Schools have found useful for students taking G.C.E. examinations.

The requirements of the various Examining Boards differ, and it is hoped that the additions to my earlier book will make this one more useful not only to Technical Schools but to Grammar Schools with a Science or Technical side.

The title is a reminder that a command of English is as essential to the scientist and technician as it is to the student of arts or commerce. Without clear exposition and explanation there is no understanding of the new knowledge coming from the world's laboratories and research stations. We all want to know about these new discoveries, and it is interesting to see firms abandoning their former reticence and using advertising space to tell us as simply as possible about a new alloy or fabric or engine.

In the factory or workshop men are no longer content merely to pull levers or tend machines. They want to know how the machine works and what it does. Schools of Apprentices or Trainees make a point nowadays of giving some idea of theory as well as imparting practical instruction. The apprentice is expected to discuss theoretical ideas and he encounters a fundamental difficulty, the inability to find the right words—or, to put it bluntly, he cannot speak or write English sufficiently well for his purpose. It must no longer be a common cry of the skilled labourer or craftsman—" I'm all right until they give me a pen and paper—then I'm finished."

The future is with those who have not only the scientific and technical knowledge but also the command of English to express it.

I am much indebted for advice and help to Mr. W. H. H. Lane

and Mr. L. F. Virgo of Whitwood Mining and Technical College, Castleford, to Mr. T. W. Houghton of Wakefield Technical College and to Mr. T. Platt of the Bristol Aeroplane Company who did the drawings.

T.H.H.

April, 1955

ACKNOWLEDGMENTS

For permission to print extracts from copyright works acknowledgments are gratefully made to the authors (or copyright owners) and publishers as follows:

F. Hoyle, *The Nature of the Universe* (Basil Blackwell); John Moore, *Portrait of Elmbury* (Collins); G. M. Trevelyan, *Clio, A Muse* and *English Social History* (Longmans Green); Robert Lynd, *Further Essays* (Dent); W. H. Hudson, *A Shepherd's Life* (Methuen); T. R. Glover, *The Ancient World* (C.U.P.); A. M. Low, *Science in Industry* (O.U.P.); P. Hood, *The Atmosphere* (Clarendon Press); E. G. O. Ridgewell and The General Electric Company, Ltd.; J. H. Jones, *The Structure of Industry* (Sampson, Low, Marston & Co.); The Editor of *The Times*; Sir Ian Jacob; Graham Hutton, *We Too Can Prosper* (Allen & Unwin); Bristol Aeroplane Company, Ltd.; K. Simpson, *Penguin Science News 4*; Arnold Toynbee, *The Teaching of History in a Shrinking World* (article in the *Spectator*).

Acknowledgment is here also made for the courteous permission granted by the following bodies to use questions from their examinations:—

University of Durham School Examinations.
The Joint Matriculation Board.
The Senate of the University of London.
The Oxford and Cambridge Examination Board.
Associated Examinations Board.
West Riding County Council.
The Institution of Civil Engineers.
The Institution of Electrical Engineers.
The Royal Society of Arts.

CONTENTS

PAGE

PART ONE : VOCABULARY . . . . . .

ON USING A DICTIONARY 1

VOCABULARY EXERCISES 2

PREFIXES AND SUFFIXES 10

PART TWO : GRAMMAR

STYLE AND USAGE 14

EXERCISES 18

PART THREE : ANALYSIS

CLAUSE-ANALYSIS 25

EXERCISES IN ANALYSIS 32

THE PHRASE 37

PART FOUR : PUNCTUATION 39

PUNCTUATION EXERCISES 41

PART FIVE : FIGURES OF SPEECH . . . 46

EXERCISES 52

PART SIX : COMPOSITION

JOINING SENTENCES 58

DESCRIPTIONS AND REPORTS 60

PAIRS 65

WHY ? 66

COLLOQUIALISMS 67

DEFINITIONS 68

SIMPLIFICATION AND MODERNISATION . . 69

REASONING 71

STATISTICAL DIAGRAMS AND GRAPHS . . 72

REPORTED SPEECH 74

LETTERS 77

THE WRITING OF AN ESSAY 82

SUBJECTS FOR ESSAYS 86

PART SEVEN : PRÉCIS WRITING . . . 94

PASSAGES FOR PRÉCIS 98

CONTENTS

PAGE

PART EIGHT : COMPREHENSION
    I. ELMBURY—JOHN MOORE 126
    II. SESAME AND LILIES—JOHN RUSKIN . . 127
    III. CLIO : A MUSE—G. M. TREVELYAN . . 128
    IV. ENGLISH SOCIAL HISTORY—G. M. TREVELYAN . 130
    V. PERSONAL JOURNALS—CAPTAIN R. F. SCOTT . 132
    VI. I TREMBLE TO THINK—ROBERT LYND . . 134
    VII. SCIENCE AND CRIME DETECTION—K. SIMPSON . 135
    VIII. ELECTRICITY TO-DAY—T. B. VINYCOMB . 137
    IX. CHILD'S PLAY—R. L. STEVENSON . . 138
    X. A SHRINKING WORLD—ARNOLD TOYNBEE . 140
    XI. TRAVELS WITH A DONKEY—R. L. STEVENSON . 142
    XII. ELEGY IN A COUNTRY CHURCHYARD—GRAY . 143
    XIII. A SHEPHERD'S LIFE—W. H. HUDSON . . 145
    XIV. POEM—A. H. CLOUGH 148
    XV. THE ANCIENT WORLD—T. R. GLOVER . . 149

Part One: *VOCABULARY*

ON USING A DICTIONARY

A dictionary is an essential reference book for educated people. It gives the spelling, meaning, pronunciation and derivation of words.

Yet surprisingly few people use a dictionary. Some seem ashamed to do so, but nobody can be, or would wish to be, a " walking dictionary ", and it is better to consult a dictionary than show ignorance by spelling " receipt " with the ' i ' before the ' e ' in an important letter.

Many people, however, are afraid to use a dictionary. They have tried before and the dictionary seemed to confuse rather than help. When first you bought a camera you needed instruction in how to use it, and at first made mistakes, until practice has now made you quite competent. So with a dictionary you need instruction and practice.

A dictionary will tell you how to spell difficult words such as :—

chrysanthemum, embarrass, interrogate

That is its simplest use, but even in this some patience is needed. It will not help to throw away the dictionary as useless just because you have failed to find " chrysanthemum " beginning with " cry ".

Now, for the other uses of a dictionary, let us look up " interrogate ".

intĕ·rrogate, v.t. Ask questions of (person &c.), esp. closely or formally. So **intĕ·rrogat**OR n. [f.L INTER (*rogare* ask), see -ATE].

Don't be discouraged. After all, when you bought that camera you did not expect to be taking colour photographs in the first week. So let us see what we can make of it.

First, the meaning—to ask questions of a person—is clear enough.

Then the attempt to tell you how to pronounce it is not too difficult. With the help of a note at the beginning of the dictionary and with practice, you learn that ' ĕ ' means that the letter ' e ' is a short vowel as in ' met ', and that the dot between the ' ĕ ' and ' r ' indicates a short pause after ' ĕ '.

Finally in the brackets at the end is the derivation of the word—from the Latin *rogare*—ask. If you are not interested it does not matter very much. Nor need you worry about v.t. (verb transitive). If you don't know the grammatical terms, you can manage without them. Just take from the dictionary what is helpful, and with practice that will be more and more.

To use this book with profit you will need a dictionary and I venture to suggest one or two of the many good dictionaries available at any bookshop.

BLACKIE : STANDARD DICTIONARY.

CHAMBERS'S TWENTIETH CENTURY DICTIONARY.

CONCISE OXFORD DICTIONARY.

OXFORD POCKET DICTIONARY.

NUTTALL'S DICTIONARY.

EXERCISE

The following paragraph has been abstracted from a dictionary :

iron, īern, *n.* (A. Sax. *iren*) A metal ; an instrument made of iron ; a utensil that when heated is used for smoothing cloth ; *pl* fetters ; chains.—*a.* Made of iron ; resembling iron, either really or metaphorically ; hence harsh, severe. —*v.t.* To smooth with an iron ; to fetter.

Explain the paragraph in detail.

R.S.A.

1.—Give verbs corresponding to (e.g., practical : practise)—

(a) bequest, utility, dew, prophet, abominable, culture, abstinence, putrid, example, certain.

(b) bitter, gulf, body, moist, beauty, noble, witch, rich, power, head.

2.—Give an adjective corresponding to—
nonsense, question, mutiny, error, crisis, defence, joke, money, vehicle, spectacle.

3.—Use in a sentence each of these adjectives, followed by a suitable noun—

 (a) temperate, auburn, amicable, pungent, conflicting, fraudulent, uniform, fervent, current, casual.

 (b) penal, mosaic, primary, luxuriant, stentorian, sedentary, illicit, rapt, exhaustive, voracious.

 (c) libellous, decisive, grotesque, placid, permanent, extinct, intrinsic, glib, hysterical, deciduous.

4.—Give two meanings for—
fast, prime, carriage, abstract, hail, smack, kind, wound, invalid, pitch.

5.—Explain the difference between—

 (a) compliment—complement ; canvas—canvass ; route—rout ; human—humane ; moral—morale ; urban—urbane ; artist—artiste.

 (b) loath—loathe ; cession—session ; deprecate—depreciate ; industrious—industrial ; hypocritical—hypercritical ; suit—suite ; antidote—anecdote.

6.—With what part of the body are the following adjectives associated ? On what occasions would these adjectives be used ?
capital, aural, optical, dorsal, pedal, nasal, mental, dental, cordial, lingual, manual, digital.

7.—Give a word of exactly opposite meaning, avoiding the use of negative prefixes and suffixes. It must be the same part of speech as the word given.

 (a) harmony, complex, severe, hostile, guilt, transparent, attractive, lazy, variety, productive.

 (b) certainty, abundance, reckless, eager, admit, oriental, assent, assemble, civilised, knowledge.

8.—(a) Write the following words in the plural :
axis, dynamo, maximum, ray, step-son.

    (b) Write the following words in the singular :
        phenomena, porches, brethren, fish, scarves.

    (c) Give the masculine form of :—
        ewe, spinster, governess, bride, marchioness, cow,
        bee, madam, bitch, landlady.

                                                  R.S.A.

9.—Give single words for—

    (a) before the dawn of history ; belonging to the Middle
        Ages ; before the Flood ; capable of more than one
        meaning ; to make a god of ; fit to eat ; quite certain
        to happen ; having a circular base and a pointed top ;
        having no equal, like or parallel ; easily moved to
        anger.

    (b) at the same moment ; a person who walks in his sleep ;
        an inscription on a tombstone ; eating flesh-meat ;
        not bearing on the actual question ; equally at home
        on land or in water ; equally capable with either hand :
        star knowledge ; conscientious even in very small
        matters ; an additional clause modifying a will.

10.—Explain the meaning of these expressions with special
        reference to the force of the adjective—

    (a) Prime Minister, Foreign Office, nice distinction,
        unanimous decision, sanitary inspector, social history,
        territorial waters, current affairs, primary school,
        secondary school.

    (b) classical education, gilt-edged security, general prac-
        titioner, sweeping statement, moral victory, interim
        report, critical attitude, civil servant, salutary effect,
        indifferent success.

11.—Explain the meaning of—
        democracy, aristocracy, plutocracy, bureaucracy, mon-
        archy, autocracy, anarchy, oligarchy, hierarchy.

12.—From these words, choose one suitable for use in the
        following sentences. Do not use the same word twice—
        stare, discover, distinguish, spy, survey, scan, inspect,
        observe, peep, peer.

(a) He refused to — upon his fellow-workers.
(b) It is difficult to — between mauve and purple.
(c) Mary tried to — over the hedge.
(d) They had come to England to — our methods of dyeing.
(e) It is considered rude to — at people.
(f) Mr. Johnson was sent to — a new site for a hospital.
(g) She seemed to — at me through her spectacles.
(h) I was never able to — who cut the rope.
(i) A man has come to — the drains.
(j) The castaway every morning climbed a hill to — the horizon.

13.—Similarly make sentences with these verbs (any form of the verb is allowed)—
(a) " Walking " verbs.
   saunter, stroll, wander, march, trudge, roam, plod, patrol, stalk, tramp.
(b) " Joining " verbs.
   unite, connect, bind, graft, tether, grapple, rivet, dove-tail, splice, strap.
(c) " Saying " verbs.
   affirm, announce, confirm, proclaim, state, hint, suggest, whisper, assert, shout.
(d) " Strong " adjectives.
   vigorous, stout, robust, hardy, mighty, sturdy, stalwart, sinewy, impregnable, invincible.
(e) " Weak " adjectives.
   feeble, frail, fragile, rickety, infirm, flimsy, rotten, decayed, decrepit, languid.
(f) " Laughter " nouns.
   smile, grin, giggle, titter, roar, chuckle, simper, smirk, guffaw, snigger.
(g) " Gift " nouns.
   donation, subscription, legacy, boon, gratuity, allowance, subsidy, alms, tribute, largesse.

14.—Use these phrases in sentences, putting in the correct preposition—

an exception — the rule ; a liking — fast bowling ;
a great likeness — his brother ; to show gratitude —
him — his kindness ; to be a slave — a habit ; proud
— his success ; oblivious — his surroundings ; worthy
— the highest praise ; apologise — your lateness ;
anxious — your safety ; favourable — his plan ; abide
— his decision ; different — all others ; ignorant — his
intentions ; triumph — difficulties.

15.—Write three sentences using the verb, in any tense,
followed by three different prepositions.
take, fall, stand, bring, write.

16.—Put **affect** or **effect** in these sentences—
(a) The loss of Jones may — the result of the match.
(b) Nothing will — my decision.
(c) The drug may — a change in the condition of the patient.
(d) With your help he will — his escape.

17.—Put the appropriate form of **awake** or **wake** in these
sentences—
(a) You will — the baby.
(b) Christians —, salute the happy morn.
(c) The alarm — me at seven o'clock.
(d) You are likely to get a rude —.
(e) — up, lazybones.
(f) When at last they — to the danger, it was too late.

18.—In these sentences decide upon **below, under,** or
beneath.
(a) They were fishing — the rapids.
(b) All men — fifty may be conscripted.
(c) Such a lie is — contempt.
(d) The standard of candidates this year is — the average.
(e) The boat shot — the bridge.
(f) He married — him.
(g) There is nothing new — the sun.
(h) The Tax does not apply to estates — £2,000.
(i) The temperature of the room fell — 40°.

19.—Decide upon **above** or **over** in these sentences—

(a) The churches of South Lincolnshire tower — the surrounding flat land.

(b) — the noise of battle the cry of the wounded could be heard.

(c) — a long period, the experiment will be worth while.

(d) The moon shines — the cowshed.

(e) As the aeroplane flew — our heads we could see its markings.

(f) The voice of the master could be heard — the din in the corridor.

(g) We could hear noises on the floor — ; then they seemed to be — our heads.

20.—Decide upon **allusion, illusion** or **delusion** in these sentences.

(a) He suffered from the — that he was another Napoleon.

(b) You must be under no — about such matters.

(c) We resent such a(n) — ; it is most unfair.

(d) Macbeth's " air-drawn dagger " was a(n) —.

(e) Marriage has been said to be a snare and a(n) —.

(f) He laboured under the dangerous — that all would come right in the end.

(g) When he mentioned a Great Power, everybody understood the —.

(h) The show was nothing but a(n) — for fools.

(i) The mirror created the — of ridiculous fatness.

(j) The — to his future hopes was very subtle.

21.—Decide between the alternatives offered in these sentences. The correct decision will show the right use of words often confused.

continuous

(a) In summer there was always a continual flow of water.

continuous

(b) I was annoyed by the continual dripping of a tap.

recourse
(c) As a last resource I must speak to your father.

recourse
(d) He was reluctant to have resource to such stern measures.

(e) Our bungalow in Kenya was almost hidden by the
luxurious
luxuriant grasses.

(f) The young man was evidently not accustomed to such
luxuriant
luxurious splendour.

masterly
(g) He played that stroke in a masterful fashion.
masterly
(h) His masterful manner made it difficult for him to com-
promise.

practice
(i) We shall see you tonight at the choir practise.
practice
(j) We are going to practise a new cantata.
practice
(k) New doctors will not now buy a practise.
licence
(l) We must remember to buy a wireless license.
licence
(m) The magistrates agreed to license the new premises.
accessary
(n) He was charged with being an accessory before the fact.
accessary
(o) A waterproof cape is a useful accessory to a cyclist's outfit.
prophecy
(p) They prophesy that he will be king.
prophecy
(q) Macbeth believed the prophesy of the witches.
contemptible
(r) Do not be contemptuous of the efforts of the inex-
perienced.
contemptible
(s) The boy proved to be a contemptuous little thief.

22.—Choose **Six** of the following pairs of words. Use each of the words in a separate sentence so as to bring out clearly the difference in meaning within each pair :
(i) stratagem, strategy ; (ii) observance, observation ; (iii) incite, insight ; (iv) recourse, resource ; (v) imaginary, imaginative ; (vi) emancipated, emaciated ; (vii) precede, proceed.

J.M.B.

23.—Choose **Eight** words from the following list and write a sentence about the nature and use of each :
lathe ; alloy ; brace ; dynamo ; volt ; duralumin ; cast-iron ; pylon ; carburettor ; clutch.

24.—Write the following words and underline that part of each word on which the principal stress of the voice falls when the word is spoken. (e.g. ab<u>surd</u>.)

(a) advocate, personnel, emigrate, photographic, inevitable, envelop, humane, mischievous, sever, transference.

(b) philosophy, advertisement, decent, admirable, condescend, precedent, a permit, evident, to convict, reconnaissance.

R.S.A.

25.—Explain carefully the meanings of **Five** of the following words and phrases, using, if possible, only one sentence in each case :—
wet blanket ; mass production ; building society ; fan mail ; zip-fastener ; crossword puzzle ; radiogram.

R.S.A.

26.—Explain briefly in one or two good sentences what sort of work is done by each of the following :
shop-walker ; purser ; dispenser ; coroner ; under-writer.

R.S.A.

27.—Choose **Six** of following words, and for each of them write **two** sentences to bring out two meanings :—
(i) converse ; (ii) defer ; (iii) lay ; (iv) invalid ; (v) refrain ; (vi) decline ; (vii) ruminate.

J.M.B.

28.—(a) Use each of the following words in two separate
sentences to show the change in meaning of the
word brought about by altering the stress from the
first to the second syllable :

incense, discount, refuse, minute.

(b) Choose **Five** of the following words. Form sentences
in which each of them is used with the appropriate
preposition :—

absolve, implicate, submit, acquit, comply, dissent,
concur, assent, different. A.E.B.

29.—Each of the following five words, in addition to its ordinary
meaning, is used in a special sense in business, industry,
etc. Write two sentences to illustrate the two uses of
each word :—

strike, duty, interest, deed, wake.

30.—Explain (a) the technical meaning and

           (b) the non-technical meaning of any **Six** of the
following words :—

acid, alcohol, balance, density, neutral, obtuse, pre-
cipitate, clutch, radiator, arterial, labyrinth, fault, levee,
articulated.

J.M.B.

PREFIXES AND SUFFIXES

The Prefix usually modifies the meaning of the word before
which it is placed. The Latin verb ducere—*to lead*, with
prefixes gives us conduct, reduce, produce.

The Suffix modifies the grammatical function of the word.
It may alter the part of speech.

e.g. From happy (adjective) we have happ*iness* (abstract
noun).

From man (noun) we have man*ly* (adjective).

From employ (verb) we have employ*er* (noun).

Suffixes may also give us feminine forms, as lion—lion*ess*,
or diminutives, as duck—duck*ling*.

LIST OF COMMON PREFIXES AND SUFFIXES

PREFIXES

(*E*=ENGLISH. *L*=LATIN. *Gk*=GREEK)

PREFIX		MEANING	EXAMPLES
A	*E*	on	aboard, aside.
AB, abs, av	*L*	from	abdicate, abscond, avert.
AD, a, ab, ac, of, ag, al, at	*L*	to	address, achieve, aggression, attract.
AMBI	*L*	⎫ on both sides,	ambidextrous.
AMPHI	*Gk*	⎭ around	amphitheatre.
ANTE, anti, anc, ant	*L*	before	antecedent, anticipate, ancient, antique.
ANTI, ant	*Gk*	against, opposite	antidote, antagonist.
ARCH, archi	*Gk*	chief	archbishop, architect.
AUTO	*Gk*	self	automobile, automatic.
BENE	*L*	well	benefit, benediction.
BI, bis	*L*	double, twice	bigamy, biscuit.
CIRCUM	*L*	round	circumference, circuit.
CON, co, col, cor, coun	*L*	together with	connect, co-operative, collect, corrode, council.
CONTRA, contro	*L*	against	contradict, controversy.
DE	*L*	down	descend.
		reversal	detach.
		intensive	declare, defile.
DIS, di, des	*L*	away, apart	discover, diverge, descant.
DUO, du	*L*	Two	dual, duplicate.
EU	*Gk*	well	euphony, euphemism.
EX, e, es	*L*	out of, very	extend, educate, escape.
FOR	*E*	intensive	forlorn, forgive.
IN, am, an, em, en	*L*	in	include, ambush, anoint, embrace, enclose.
IN, en, i, il, im, ir	*L*	not	infirm, enemy, ignoble, illegal, improper, irregular.
INTER	*L*	between	intermediate.
META	*Gk*	change	metaphor.
MICRO	*Gk*	small	microscope.
MIS	*E*	wrongly	mistake, misdeed.
MIS	*L*	badly, ill	misadventure, mischief.
MONO	*Gk*	one	monoplane, monotonous

PREFIX		MEANING	EXAMPLES
OB, oc, op	L	near, against	oblong, occur, oppress.
PAN, panto	Gk	all	Pan-American, panto-mime.
PEN	L	almost	peninsula.
PER, par, pel	L	through	perspective, parson, pellucid.
PERI	Gk	around	perimeter.
POLY	Gk	many	polygon, polytechnic.
POST	L	after, behind	postpone, post-date.
RE, red	L	again, back	renew, react, redeem.
RETRO	L	backwards	retrograde, retrospect.
SE	L	apart	separate, secret, secure.
SINE	L	without	sinecure.
SUB, su, suc, sug, sup	L	under	submarine, subscribe, sub-committee, suppress.
SUPER	L	above	superlative, supreme.
SYN, sym	Gk	together with	synchronise, sympathy.
TELE	Gk	far	telescope, television.
TRANS	L	across	transfer, transparent.
TRI	L	thrice	triangle, triple, treble.
UN	E	not	unmanly.
		reverse the action	undo, untie.
UN, uni	L	one	unanimous, uniform
VICE	L	in place of	vice-captain, viceroy.

SUFFIXES

A list of common suffixes would be so long as to be confusing ; but here are a few :

ess—forms feminine : tigress, abbess.

ic—mainly scientific terms : atomic, arithmetic.

ment—Nouns from Verbs : argument, settlement.

er, or, ar, ant, ent—Nouns (action or occupation) : merchant, farmer, sailor, scholar, student.

ling, let, icle—diminutives : duckling, gosling, rivulet, hamlet, icicle.

hood, ness, ship—Abstract Nouns : childhood, goodness, friendship.

EXERCISES

1.—Give the meaning of these words, bringing out the force
of the prefix :

(a) bicycle, counterfeit, transplant, automatic, ignoble,
polygon, superlative, precede.

(b) foresight, postscript, circumference, international, per-
fume, dispel, bigamy, aftermath.

(c) absent, deluge, monogram, adhesive, transport, di-oxide,
forsake, subtract.

(d) monotony, duet, tripod, quadruped, quinquereme, pen-
tagon, hexagon, heptagon, octopus, December.

2.—By adding a prefix give the opposite of :
bolt, claim, courteous, known, liberal, mount, noble,
perfect, sense, moderate, legible, mortal, efficient, natural,
mature.

3.—In each of the following words one element is underlined.
Give the meaning of each word, then supply another
word containing the same element and give the meaning
of the word you have supplied.
autograph, microscope, antidote, antecedent, inflam-
mable, panorama.
J.M.B.

4.—Add a suffix to each of the following, and state what change
in the meaning or function of the word has been made.
act, hate, witch, picture, king, hope, free, fortune,
infant, china.

5.—What is the force of the suffix in each of these words ?
darling, cigarette, colliery, senseless, Johnson, usage,
mistress, milliner, justice, farthing.

6.—By means of suffixes form adjectives from the following
words :
burden, forget, spasm, profession, man ; and afterwards
use the adjectives in sentences so as to show their
meaning.

Part Two: GRAMMAR

STYLE AND USAGE

1.—Agreement of Subject and Verb.

(a) Two or more subjects joined by "and" take a plural verb.

e.g. You and I are going.

If two subjects are joined by " or (nor) ", the verb agrees with the nearer subject.

e.g. A rubber or two of bridge were played before supper.
Either you or I am wrong.

N.B.—It is better to avoid this difficulty by repeating the verb.

Either you are wrong or I am.

(b) Subjects used distributively (i.e., a number of subjects taken one at a time) take a singular verb.

e.g. Each of us has a shilling.
Neither of the boxers was satisfied with the decision.
Many a boy has been helped by the generosity of the Founder of this school.

Note the difference between " each other ", " one another ".
In the duel they killed each other (two persons).
In the mist our soldiers were killing one another (more than two persons).

(c) Collective Nouns are the names of collections of things and, when they are considered as a whole, take a singular verb.

e.g. The football team is to be photographed.
The crowd was angry.
The jury has just retired.

But if these nouns are considered as a number of separate persons, then a plural verb is needed.

e.g. The crowd were throwing up their hats.
The jury have agreed on their verdict.

A number of boys were caught in the orchard.

ALL—NONE: The verb after **all** and **none** may be singular or plural, according to the sense.

e.g. All are waiting for the signal.

Come home : all is forgiven.

It is not surprising that none have heard of it.

Of those invited to the reception, none was more proud than I.

2.—**Case.**

(a) The verb **" To Be "** takes the same case after it as before it.

e.g. It was *he* who did it.

I know that man to be *him*.

In conversation we accept " It's me ", and we should consider " It is I " pedantic in answer to the question " Who's there ? "

(b) The Objective (Accusative) Case is necessary (i) for the object of a verb ; (ii) following a preposition.

e.g. *Whom* do you seek ?

This is just between *you* and *me*.

But (except) is a preposition.

e.g. There's nobody but *me* at home.

Sometimes it is preferable to consider " but " as a conjunction, especially if the following pronoun is followed by a verb.

e.g. Nobody but *he* would have done such a thing.

The boy stood on the burning deck

Whence all but *he* had fled.

(c) The Relative Pronoun takes its case from its function in the clause in which it stands.

e.g. This is the man *who* did it.

This is the man *whom* the police suspect.

We chose Jones *who* we thought would be a good captain.

i.e. We thought *he* would be a good captain.

We chose Jones *whom* we thought likely to be a good captain.

3.—The Verb.

(a) Shall and Will. (Should and would). The rule is : use " shall " for first person, singular and plural, and " will (wilt) " for second and third persons, if the idea expressed is simply that something is going to happen in the future.

e.g. I shall go to Manchester tomorrow ; will you come with me ?

If, however, some compulsion, determination or prohibition is meant, then the rule is reversed : " will " for first person, " shall (shalt) " for second and third persons.

e.g. Thou shalt not steal.
We will not give in.
I shall drown and nobody will save me (accident).
I will drown and nobody shall save me (suicide).

(b) The Unrelated Participial Phrase.
Take care not to leave a participial phrase without a logical subject.

e.g. Having ceased raining, he decided to set out at once.
When riding in a train, stationary objects appear to be in motion.
Coming up the hill, the sun was on our left. (Change this to : As we came up the hill, the sun was on our left.)

(c) The Present Participle and the Gerund are often confused.

e.g. (A note from a parent to a teacher). Please excuse Tommy leaving early today. " Leaving " is a present participle, agreeing with " Tommy ", and the sentence means : Please excuse Tommy who is leaving early today. The parent does not mean this ; it is Tommy's " leaving early " or " early departure " that is to be excused.

Correct to : Please excuse Tommy's leaving early today. " Leaving " is a Gerund (Verb-Noun) and should be preceded by the possessive form of the noun or pronoun.

e.g. I don't like *your* taking such a risk.
He was surprised at *my* coming.
There is little chance of *their* agreeing.

4.—Due : Owing.

" Due " is to be used adjectivally :
e.g. We always treat him with due respect.
The accident was due to his defective brakes.
" Owing " is to be used adjectivally, or adverbially :
e.g. The accident was owing to his defective brakes.
Owing to his defective brakes, there was an accident.
It is a common error to say :
Due to his defective brakes, there was an accident.

5.—Elementary Faults that Persist.

(a) LIE—LAY.

	Present	*Past*	*Perfect*
lie, (rest, recline,)	I lie.	I lay.	I have lain.
lay (place, arrange, deposit)	I lay.	I laid.	I have laid.

e.g. I lay still and waited.
The mayor laid the foundation stone.
Hens do not lay well in winter.

(b) ITS—IT'S.
The possessive pronouns (its, ours, hers, yours, theirs) do not take an apostrophe.
e.g. The fox has lost its tail.
But : It's a long way. (It's = It is.)

(c) MAY—CAN.
BOY : " Please, sir, can I borrow a rubber ? "
MASTER : " Yes, and you may."

6.—Ambiguity.

A sentence which may have two meanings is ambiguous.
Ambiguity is a common error of style.
e.g. Troops sent to flood area (newspaper headline).

Jones has not been bowling for many overs.

Mary loved John more than anyone.

Ambiguity may be caused by (i) the wrong order of words.

e.g. He only works when he has no money.

Your coat wants mending badly.

(ii) the vague use of pronouns.

e.g. Before giving the baby milk, boil it.

" and when they arose early in the morning, behold, they were all dead corpses." (2 Kings xix, 35.)

7.—Tautology.

Another fault of style is tautology, the use of unnecessary words.

e.g. It is just exactly ten minutes to two (omit " just " or " exactly ").

The Opposition again made another attack on the Bill.

The girl was equally as foolish as her sister.

8.—Unique.

" Unique " means the only one of its kind in existence. Therefore it is wrong to say " more unique " or " most unique ". Other words that cannot be compared are : full, complete, chief, ideal.

9.—Literally.

" Literally " means exactly to the letter. It is often misused, as here :

It was literally raining cats and dogs.

Australia is literally hungry for the right type of emigrant.

EXERCISES

Correct these sentences. Briefly give a reason for the correction.

1. (a) I wonder if it was her.

(b) Neither of you are very good singers.

(c) Who shall we send ?

(d) He is one of the few players I know who plays that shot well.

(e) What our team wants are five new forwards.

(f) Seated on the top of a camel, the eye of the Arab watched the horizon.

(g) He is a better cricketer than I have ever seen.

(h) Either of the men were eligible for re-election.

2. (a) Not being used to the climate, the appointment was not suitable for him.

(b) We never reached our target, due chiefly to the lack of sufficient collectors.

(c) Neither the lorry nor the trailer are fit to be on the road.

(d) Every boy was helping each other to do their homework.

(e) They chose Jackson, and he only in Form Five, as captain.

(f) The five forwards, cleverly passing to each other, swept down the field.

(g) The number of examination successes is fewer this year than last.

(h) The plank across the stream was loose at either end.

3. (a) The next game will be played by you and I.

(b) Having died on the mountain, we buried him there.

(c) The Act has been passed that the sick can receive free medical attention.

(d) I wish I could afford to dress like you do.

(e) There are a set of chessmen in that box.

(f) Between each post there is a space of three yards.

(g) I can never rely on him doing the right thing.

(h) The reason my daughter was absent is because she had a cold.

4. (a) The last place is between you three.

(b) He was stood at the corner of the street.

(c) What is the use of me doing this ?

(d) Patrons who find our waiters disrespectful should see the manager.

(e) Largely through single putts, a crowd of Ulstermen, who had hurried over by steam packet, saw their man go in to lunch three up.

(f) Mary stood before the fire and looked round.

(g) For weeks he only ate rice.

5. (a) When mother went out I sat down after putting baby into the pram to fill in a crossword puzzle.

(b) The peace, which had been hardly won, was in danger.

(c) A rope of pearls hung round her neck, the value of which I am not sure.

(d) Clean an iron saucepan with a lid.

(e) Preston Library waived all fines for a week and got back one book issued in 1926.

(f) After waiting some time, one of Sampson's Luxury Coaches swung round the corner.

(g) I am not one of those who is afraid to say what I mean.

(h) He had laid where he had fallen all night.

6.—Give the meaning of each of the following sentences as it is written, and re-write each sentence so that it gives quite clearly the intended meaning.

(i) Use your own trams and buses.

(ii) Wild animals are very interesting to watch, especially if in a hidden position.

(iii) If at any time you find yourself within easy distance of my house, I hope you will stay there for the night.

(iv) Many protests have been made about the carelessness of road users, thus causing many unnecessary accidents.

7.—State which of the words in italics in each of the following sentences is correct.

(i) (*Due, owing*) to her father's death she has postponed her visit to us.

(ii) As I had a bad headache, I went upstairs and (*laid, layed, lay*) down on the bed for an hour.

(iii) Let us do each (*others', other's*) work for a change.

(iv) Between you and (*I, me*), there is some doubt about his honesty.

(v) I object to (*your, you're, you*) going by yourself.

(vi) If I had ever uttered such a statement, I (*shall, should, would*) deserve to be punished.

(vii) One must be patient and wait (*our, his, one*'s) turn.

J.M.B.

8. (a) Point out and correct the mistake in each of the following five sentences :

   (i) After the day's shooting was over, I gave the dog it's dinner.

  (ii) He read in the papers that the man who he had run over died shortly afterwards.

 (iii) The piece of furniture was two hundred years old and very unique.

 (iv) Each of the boys have been on holiday this summer.

  (v) I told the boy that I did not like him beating the dog.

(b) Replace the slang words or phrases in each of the following sentences by good English :

   (i) By the end of the holidays he was fed up with doing nothing.

  (ii) He failed the examination through slipping up on the arithmetic paper.

 (iii) The film was wizard and we all laughed heartily.

 (iv) Working long hours was beginning to get him down, and he looked forward to his holiday.

  (v) Although very light, the boxer packed a terrific punch.

OXFORD AND CAMBRIDGE.

9. (a) There is an error in each of the following sentences. Rewrite the sentence correctly.

   (i) I am not sure as to whether he said the name was Smith or Smythe.

  (ii) He said the war was now over, he continued to say we had many difficulties ahead of us.

(iv) It is quite feasible that it may be a hot day tomorrow.

(v) If I was given the choice I would certainly prefer to go by air.

(b) Put the verbs in each of the following sentences into the past tense.

(i) I shall go up to London by the first train as I mean to be back for supper.

(ii) Suddenly a boy rushes into the house and sinks down on the sofa, panting.

(iii) How well that boy sings ; I can hardly believe my ears.

(iv) I lie down in the afternoon because the doctor insists on a daily rest.

(v) He brings me milk early so that we may breakfast at eight o'clock.

OXFORD AND CAMERIDGE

10.—Explain carefully the differences in meaning in the following pairs of sentences :

(i) I shall call to see you, whatever happens.
I will call to see you, whatever happens.

(ii) My friends love you much more than me.
My friends love you much more than I.

(iii) I wish you could hear him singing.
I wish you could hear his singing.

(iv) I wonder whether I can lift that stone.
I wonder whether I may lift that stone.

LONDON

11.—Rewrite the following sentences, and correct two mistakes in each :—

(i) My answers will be equally as good as yours, due to my hard work.

(ii) I am undecided as to whether the rug should lay there or not.

(iii) If that most unique vase was to fall off the shelf it would be a pity.

(iv) I would have liked to go, and really did ought to have gone, but I couldn't find the time.

(v) My farm is the best of the two, having given a thousand
pounds for it.

OXFORD AND CAMBRIDGE

12.—Explain precisely what is wrong in the following sentences
and rewrite them in correct and natural English.
(i) She spoke for women whom she claimed most hated
war because they suffered most from it.
(ii) That was the promised land for which he was to prepare but not to enter.
(iii) That depends on the question as to with what they
are to be cut.
(iv) It was while receiving a delegation that the bullet of
the anarchist struck the president.
(v) This is one of the few good books that has appeared
this year.

J.M.B.

13.—Point out where the ambiguity lies in each of the following sentences.
(i) Passengers must cross the line by the bridge.
(ii) Man's work ends with the setting sun ;
Woman's work is never done.
(iii) He would be the last person to come here.
(iv) I expect nothing less than to lose this election.
(v) I shall lose no time in reading your book.

J.M.B.

14.—Each of the following sentences is capable of two different
meanings. Making only slight changes, rewrite each
sentence so that it is capable of only one of the two
meanings.
(i) Did you observe the library regulations ?
(ii) The children, who wanted something more exciting to
look at than their elders, rushed to the Punch and
Judy show.
(iii) Tom told Dick he had been selected to play centre-
forward.

(iv) Girls like these stories because they are full of romantic nonsense.

(v) She was one of those curious people who are never satisfied.

(vi) I want nothing less than fame.

J.M.B.

15.—Do you find anything incorrect or slovenly in the following sentences ? Rewrite them, where necessary, in good English, and give reasons for the changes :

(i) Since the beginning of the war, eggs have been in short supply.

(ii) No-one can be easy in their minds about the prospect of good weather tomorrow.

(iii) Dear Sir,

We enclose your account to the end of May. Wishing to collect all debts due to us, will you please send us your cheque as soon as you can ?

(iv) After dinner, John felt so ill that he had to lay down.

(v) Mary made tea for my sister and I.

(vi) After his illness, he went away for three weeks holiday.

LONDON

16. (a) In each of the following sentences **one** word is used wrongly. Copy down the sentence, but with a **correct word** (or words) **substituted** ; and explain carefully the proper use of the word you have dropped from the corrected sentences.

(i) The sight of her own face literally upset her.

(ii) A unique case : I know of only two others.

(iii) The gang was decimated : only half of them escaped.

(iv) It may not always be political for a politician to say what he thinks.

(b) Point out the logical absurdity in each of the following :

(i) The dog's legs too short ? Why, he can reach the ground with them, can't he ?

(ii) It's a pity so many farms have their gates in the muddiest part of the fields.

J.M.B.

Part Three: *ANALYSIS*

CLAUSE-ANALYSIS

The **Complex Sentence** is one in which there are two or more clauses, one of which is of more importance (**Main Clause**), and the other, or others, of less importance (**Subordinate Clause**).

e.g.
 (i) They laughed when they saw him.
 (ii) Caesar said, " Shall Caesar send a lie ? "
 (iii) I have seen the house you mean.
 (iv) Wherever you are, I shall find you.

These sentences divide—

(i)	Main Clause	They laughed
	Subordinate Clause	when they saw him.
(ii)	Main Clause	Caesar said
	Subordinate Clause	" Shall Caesar send a lie ? "
(iii)	Main Clause	I have seen the house
	Subordinate Clause	you mean.
(iv)	Main Clause	I shall find you
	Subordinate Clause	wherever you are.

EXERCISES

Divide each sentence into Main and Subordinate Clauses.

(A)—

(1) I stayed for the night at an old inn which stood on a lonely moor.

(2) I had hardly dropped asleep when I was awakened by a curious noise.

(3) I wondered what it was.

(4) As I turned my head to listen I saw a light near the far wall.

(5) It gradually grew until it became a shape.

(6) Before I could speak the shape had gone.

(7) Although I was afraid, I still lay there waiting and listening.

(8) The beams of the moon, which just then emerged from behind a cloud, shone on the highly-polished wardrobe.

(9) Then I realised it was no ghost.

(10) I slept soundly until the maid brought me a morning cup of tea.

(B)—

(1) The most lovely garden I ever saw is near Ambleside.

(2) As you leave the town by the road to Langdale, look for a half-hidden gateway on the right.

(3) On the wall is a notice which invites you to enter the garden.

(4) There you may wander as you please.

(5) As it is sheltered and faces south, flowers, trees and shrubs flourish there.

(6) In June, azaleas, which seem to be of every colour, flame on the flower beds.

(7) Paths you hardly notice because you are admiring the wonderful variety of rock-plants, lead you up the hill until you reach the top.

(8) There seats are placed that you may rest.

(9) The view of Windermere which you catch on that hill is the most wonderful surprise of all.

(10) If you are in the Lake District do not miss that garden.

SUBORDINATE CLAUSES

There are three kinds of Subordinate Clauses, named, according to the work they do, Adjective Clauses, Noun Clauses, Adverb Clauses.

THE ADJECTIVE CLAUSE

The Adjective Clause does the work of an adjective, describing a noun or pronoun.

   e.g.

   (i) The Headmaster wants a list of boys *who are absent*.

   (ii) One of the chickens *you sold me* has died.

These may be analysed :

(i)	Main Clause	The Headmaster wants a list of boys
	Adjective Clause	(describes " boys ") who are absent
(ii)	Main Clause	One of the chickens has died
	Adjective Clause	(describes " chickens ") you sold me

EXERCISES

Analyse these sentences containing Adjective Clauses.

1.—

   (a) This is the house that Jack built.

   (b) The house Jack built cost over a thousand pounds.

   (c) Jack married Mary who lived in the next street.

   (d) I know the girl you mean.

   (e) They were married at the church where they met.

   (f) Jack works at a factory where chocolate is made.

   (g) Mary, who is a pretty girl, serves in a café.

   (h) The furniture they have bought is of the best quality.

   (i) They have a garden in which lovely flowers grow.

   (j) They are the happiest people I know.

2.—

   (a) All they did was well done.

   (b) I remember the time when there was rationing.

   (c) It's a long lane that has no turning.

   (d) All that glitters is not gold.

   (e) He who would have the kernel must crack the nut.

   (f) It is long past the time when you should be in bed.

   (g) This is the pen you have been looking for.

   (h) People who live in glass houses should not throw stones.

   (i) Brazil is a country where coffee is grown.

(j) It was just such a thing as I have often warned you against.

3 —Rewrite these sentences, changing the italicised words in each sentence into an Adjective Clause which gives the same meaning as, but does not contain, the italicised words.

(a) He was proud of our *invincible* team.

(b) Parliament is a *legislative* council.

(c) Yours is a *very creditable* result.

(d) He told me an *incredible* story.

(e) Some Yorkshiremen are *the most credulous* men.

(f) The rajah showed us *priceless* jewels.

(g) Taxes should never be an *intolerable* burden.

(h) He looked for shelter from the *imminent* storm.

(i) For his absence he gave a *very plausible* excuse.

(j) The teacher reproached her for her *illegible* writing.

THE NOUN CLAUSE

The Noun Clause may be the Subject, Complement or Object of a Verb ; in apposition to a Noun or Pronoun ; or following a Preposition.

e.g. *What he said* could not be heard. Noun Clause Subject.

My answer is " *I do not know*." Noun Clause Complement.

He asked *who I was*. Noun Clause Object.

There was a strong rumour *that he was leaving the town*. Noun Clause in Apposition.

He would abide by *what he said*. Noun Clause following Preposition.

EXERCISES

1.—Make Complex Sentences by adding Noun Clauses.

(a) The man exclaimed ——

(b) Peter asked ——

(c) —— cried John.

(d) The duke replied ——

(e) The king in anger roared ——
(f) —— muttered Sir Thomas.
(g) Mr. Williams said ——
(h) —— rejoined Mrs. Williams.
(i) We all wondered ——
(j) We all hoped ——

2.—In these sentences put Noun Clauses instead of the words in italics.
(a) Tell us *the news*.
(b) The police warned him *of the consequences*.
(c) He was very sorry *for his misdeeds*.
(d) I shall never forget *your kindness*.
(e) The strikers are demanding *a rise in wages*.
(f) The Mayor has promised *a subscription*.
(g) I never expected *a refusal*.
(h) The man denied *the accusation*.
(i) The prisoner affirmed *his innocence*.
(j) The best news of the week was *his success in the examination*.

3.—Analyse these sentences containing Noun Clauses.
(a) My mother says I cannot have a dog.
(b) Her reason is dogs are noisy and dirty.
(c) I could buy a dog with what I have in my money-box.
(d) I hope I shall persuade her.
(e) Some country men believe that the weather changes with the moon.
(f) How the year went by, I know not.
(g) I cannot imagine how you do such a clever trick.
(h) It has been settled that we return tomorrow.
(i) Where the ball is remains a mystery.
(j) Where the ball is nobody knows.

4.—Analyse these sentences containing Noun Clauses.
(a) You never told us you were coming.

(b) " When shall we three meet again ? " is a quotation from *Macbeth*.

(c) Let me know when you are in London.

(d) The lady asked us what was the matter.

(e) Our answer was we were hungry.

(f) I had no idea you would do such a thing (had no idea = did not imagine).

(g) I was afraid that would happen (was afraid = feared).

(h) I know little about what is happening in the next room.

(i) This youth is a stranger, I think.

(j) You never mentioned the fact that you had seen the accident.

5.—Make original sentences having Noun Clauses following these verbs :

claimed, stated, demanded, swore, explained, declared, pleaded, denied, whispered, screamed.

THE ADVERB CLAUSE

The Adverb Clause does the work of an Adverb, modifying a Verb, Adjective or Adverb.

Kinds of Adverb Clauses—

(i) You may go *when you have finished*.   (Time.)

(ii) The accident happened *where the three roads meet*.   (Place.)

(iii) He played *as only a master can*.   (Manner.)

(iv) *Because (as, since) he had no money*, he begged in the streets.   (Cause.)

(v) He tried very hard *so that he could keep his place in the form*.   (Purpose.)

(vi) He was so angry *that I was afraid of him*.   (Result.)

(vii) *If you will go to the shop*, I will give you a penny.   (Condition.)

Unless he improves, we shall drop him from the team.   (Condition.)

(viii) *Although it is raining now*, we expect fair weather later in the day.   (Concession.)

(ix) He played better *than I did*.   (Degree.)

EXERCISES

1.—Add to these Main Clauses Adverb Clauses of the kind indicated.
- (a) Mother was so pleased. (Result.)
- (b) The man laughed. (Manner.)
- (c) Mary shut her eyes. (Purpose.)
- (d) John cried out. (Cause.)
- (e) The boy is not eligible. (Condition.)
- (f) He is in the Sixth Form. (Concession.)
- (g) Baby is as happy. (Degree.)
- (h) I will stop. (Time.)
- (i) The bus will stop. (Place.)
- (j) I will hit you. (Condition.)

2.—Analyse these sentences containing Adverb Clauses.
- (a) When you have decided let me know.
- (b) I have not seen him since he came back from his holidays.
- (c) He has gone where the bad boys go.
- (d) They laughed when I said that.
- (e) One laughed so much that he nearly choked.
- (f) He drove the car as if he were drunk.
- (g) I can whistle more sweetly than I can sing.
- (h) If you have finished you may go.
- (i) You must finish before you go.
- (j) Don't go unless you wish.

3.—Analyse these sentences containing Adverb Clauses.
- (a) The detective shadowed the suspect wherever he went.
- (b) Come when you like.
- (c) I shall expect you to play even if it is in the second team.
- (d) If he were not so selfish he would be a good centre-forward.
- (e) He was very careful lest they should learn his secret.
- (f) If you wish I will help you.
- (g) Before the week was over I was tired of the place.
- (h) John overtook me as I was walking down the street.

(i) You may season the dish as you please.
(j) As I was busy I could not come then.

EXERCISES IN ANALYSIS

Divide these sentences into clauses, name the clauses and state their relationship to each other.

1.—
(a) John hoped that his escape had not been noticed.
(b) If he could reach the woods he would feel safe.
(c) There the undergrowth was so thick that it would be easy to hide.
(d) It was fortunate that the enemy had not searched him.
(e) The paper he carried was hidden in the heel of his left boot.
(f) He wondered whether the Maquis would believe his story.
(g) So many spies had been found that every stranger was feared.
(h) When darkness had fallen he crossed the road.
(i) He kept near the hedge which skirted the field.
(j) Before the moon rose he was safely under cover of some brambles.

2.—
(a) The newspapers reported that the club had transferred Jones, the full back.
(b) It was said that the fee was a record.
(c) Supporters who had been loyal for years naturally grumbled.
(d) They asked why the player had gone.
(e) The directors decided that an explanation should be made.
(f) The next Saturday, when spectators opened their programmes, they learned the truth.
(g) The player had asked for a transfer because his wife's health was not good.
(h) A doctor had recommended that a change of air would be beneficial.

(i) Although they did not wish to lose him, they must let him go.

(j) That was the reason why the player had been transferred.

3.—

(a) The master said the boy was lazy and he would not be surprised if he failed the examination.

(b) The announcement that the King would present the medals gave great happiness to those who were to receive them.

(c) As I waited for the arrival of Antonio I thought of the many happy days we had spent together when we were young.

(d) The girl was so proud of her red shoes that she wore them whenever she went out.

(e) What became of my companions in the boat as well as those who escaped on the rock I cannot tell, but conclude they were all lost.

(f) Before you go any further, I would like to ask if you have considered how much all this will cost.

(g) The news that he had been assassinated was spread through the city by those who were plotting a rising.

(h) Gerard seized the mad fellow's arm in dismay, for he had been long enough in the country to guess that the whole town would take part in any brawl with a native against a stranger.

(i) I will let you know what I have done that you may be ready for whatever may happen in the days that lie ahead.

(j) When we were alone in the fields he talked with me so earnestly that I had no doubt that the information he gave was true.

4.—The conversation, which was at a high pitch of animation when Silas approached the door of the Rainbow, had, as usual, been slow and intermittent when the company first assembled. The pipes began to be puffed in a silence which had an air of severity ; the more important

B*

customers, who drank spirits and sat nearest the fire, stared at each other as if a bet were depending on the first man who winked.

5.—Mr. Weller had, at that time, no further opportunity of dwelling on the apprehensions which beset his mind, for the immediate occasion of his fears proceeded to lead the way downstairs, apologising as they went for conducting him into the kitchen, which apartment, however, she was induced to proffer for his accommodation in preference to her little room, the rather as it afforded greater facilities for smoking, and was immediately adjoining the ale-cellar.

6.—Combine the following sentences in three different ways, as different from one another as possible.

(a) I had never been to London before. I enjoyed myself very much.

(b) We arrived late at the field. The match had not begun.

(c) Mary had never been to the dentist's before. She could not help feeling afraid.

7.—Expand the simple sentence :—The general ordered an attack at dawn.—by the addition of an Adverb Clause of Concession, a participial phrase, an Adjective Clause.

8.—Construct sentences, each having a different subordinate clause beginning with " that " to introduce—

(a) Noun Clause Object.

(b) Adjective Clause.

(c) Adverb Clause of Result.

(d) Noun Clause in Apposition.

9.—Construct three sentences containing the clause " when the train arrived " as—

(a) Noun Clause.

(b) Adjective Clause.

(c) Adverb Clause.

10.—Without changing the meaning, replace the italicised

words in each sentence by a subordinate clause.
State the kind and function of each clause.

(a) The rumour *of his death* was untrue.
(b) *Despite his injured leg* he played well.
(c) He is a batsman of *great promise*.
(d) *To obtain entrance to the ruins* you must apply at the
     farmhouse.
(e) He asked *about my father's health*.
(f) The document proved *the prisoner's innocence*.
(g) *In his absence* he was found guilty of many crimes.
(h) I will help you *to the best of my ability*.
(i) The jury assembled to determine *the cause of death*.
(j) *His opinion on the question* was awaited by us all.

II.—

(a) Use the word **where** to introduce—
     (i) a simple sentence.
     (ii) a dependent adverb clause.
     (iii) a dependent adjectival clause.
     (iv) a dependent noun clause.
(b) Write six sentences using—
     (i) *still* as a verb.
     (ii) *still* as a noun.
     (iii) *still* as an adjective.
     (iv) *still* as an adverb.
     (v) *well* as an adverb.
     (vi) *well* as a verb.   J.M.B.

12.—

(a) Analyse the following sentence into clauses, naming each
     subordinate clause and showing its relation to the
     clause on which it depends :—
     The moon sheds so much light, and seems so bright, that
     it is often difficult to remember that the moon has no
     light except that which falls on it from the sun.
(b) Rewrite each of the following complex sentences as a
     simple sentence.
     (i) As he knew nothing about the subject which was being

discussed he decided that he had better remain silent.
(ii) Every human being indulges in some hobby which has some peculiar and absorbing interest for him.

DURHAM

13.—Combine the following simple statements in such a way as to form a continuous narrative made up of **two** complex sentences :—

William Penn was a Quaker. He founded a colony among the American Indians. He determined to treat them with kindness and justice. He took land from them. He paid for the land. The Indians once made an agreement with him. They would take English goods. They would give some land for the goods. The land was to be a certain size. A young man was to be able to walk round it in a day.

LONDON

14.—

(a) Analyse the following passage into clauses, showing their kind, and, where necessary, dependence or relation :

When I visited the old town, the house in which my father was born was still standing, but it seemed very shabby. It was evident, however, that the occupant enjoyed sunning himself in that quiet garden.

(b) Give from the passage above **one** example of each of the following :—

(i) a reflexive pronoun.
(ii) a relative pronoun.
(iii) a co-ordinating conjunction.
(iv) a possessive adjective.
(v) a present participle.
(vi) a past participle.
(vii) an auxiliary verb.
(viii) a preposition.
(ix) an adverb of degree.
(x) an adverb of time.
(xi) an adjective used predicatively (i.e. as complement).

J.M.B.

THE PHRASE

A Phrase is a group of words which does not contain a Finite Verb, and therefore does not form a sentence. Phrases may be classified according to the work they do in a sentence.

Noun Phrases.

    (i) *How to make ends meet* is our problem.   (Subject.)

    (ii) I would like *to play the piano*.   (Object.)

    (iii) Johnson, *our best player*, was my partner.   (in Apposition.)

    (iv) My intention is *to tell the truth*.   (Complement.)

Adjective Phrases.

    (i) It is a matter *of no importance*.   (des. " matter ".)

    (ii) The farmer caught the boys *stealing apples*.   (des. " boys ".)

    (iii) *Armed with an umbrella*, the woman attacked the intruder.   (des. " woman ".)

    (iv) I will show you the way *to do it*.   (des. " way ".)

Adverb Phrases.

    (i) The poachers went *through the wood*.   (Place.)

    (ii) *By skilful play* he defeated his opponent.   (Manner.)

    (iii) I have come *to see your drawings*.   (Purpose.)

    (iv) *My homework done*, I went to the pictures.   (Time.)

EXERCISES

1.—To what part of speech is each of the italicised phrases equivalent ? Point out the word on which each depends, and state its relationship to that word.

(a) *To avoid trouble in future*, please be more careful.

(b) Their request *to have their grievances considered* was refused.

(c) *To score the winning goal* is the ambition of every schoolboy.

(d) The proposal *to change from association football to rugby* was warmly debated.

(e) I am sorry *to hear of his death*.

(f) He was found guilty of *helping the enemy*.

(g) The reason *for doing this* must be explained.

(h) We saw you *running home from school*

(i) Who taught you *to play the violin ?*

(j) Jesus, *seeing the multitude,* had compassion on them.

2.—To what part of speech is each of the italicised phrases in the following sentences equivalent? Point out the word on which each depends, and state its relation to that word.

(a) We have met to-day *to consider the report of our sub-committee.*

(b) I ask you *to consider the report very carefully.*

(c) The report contains suggestions *of the very greatest importance.*

(d) It is important *to come to a decision* at the earliest possible moment.

(e) The proposal *to nationalise the railways* was certain to meet with strong opposition.

J.M.B.

3.—

(a) " People of wide reading and culture will talk unconcernedly of an Ionic cross, confusing Celts of the dark ages with Greeks of the time of Pericles." Copy down the adjectives or adjective phrases which describe—

    (i) people.

    (ii) cross.

    (iii) Celts.

(b) " This book tries to show in a simple way how the form of buildings *in different periods* was due to the materials in use and to the special purpose of a building."

  (i) Copy down—

    (a) a noun clause, saying to what verb it is attached ;

    (b) an adverb phrase of manner, saying what word it modifies.

  (ii) Explain to what part of speech the phrase in italics is equivalent, and its function in the sentence.

J.M.B.

Part Four: *PUNCTUATION*

Punctuation, or the correct use of stops, is an important part of composition. Its purpose is clearness ; the right stops enable the reader to see quickly the words in their proper groups, and thus to understand what the writer means.

The difference made by punctuation can be seen in this sentence :

Do you know John asked Albert.

This may be punctuated with very different meanings.

" Do you know John ? " asked Albert.

Do you know John asked Albert ?

" Do you know ? " John asked Albert.

Many of you will remember how Peter Quince " rid his prologue like a rough colt ; he knows not the stop ", (" A Midsummer Night's Dream ", Act v, Sc.1) and said just the opposite of what he meant.

The use of the Full Stop, Exclamation Mark, Question Mark and Inverted Commas is largely mechanical and should raise little difficulty at this stage ; but many pupils have only vague ideas about the use of Commas, while the Semi-Colon and Colon are often quite unknown.

The Comma is the stop most often used, and for that reason most often misused. As many commas are optional and may be omitted or included according to personal taste, it is not easy to satisfy those who ask for rules. They will learn from practice rather than from rules ; but these points may help.

1.—The most useful commas are " bracket " commas. Just as brackets are used in Mathematics, so " bracket " commas group together words and phrases to be thought of as separate from the main sense of the sentence. These " bracket " commas must, of course, go in pairs ; there must be two ends to the bracket.
   e.g.

(a) Fox and Davis, the opening batsmen, played steadily.

(b) The King and Queen, accompanied by Princess Elizabeth and Princess Margaret, left by train last night for Balmoral.

(c) Please, Jones, will you fetch me a paper ?

2.—Note these sentences :

(a) The man who committed the crime has been arrested.

(b) The man, who came from Nelson, confessed his guilt.

If you can understand why there are no commas in (a) and two commas in (b) you have not much to learn about the use of commas.   In (a) the person arrested is " the man who committed the crime," i.e. " the wanted man " or the " guilty man ".   The adjective clause " who committed the crime " is an essential, defining clause.

In (b) the clause " who came from Nelson " may be interesting, especially to readers from East Lancashire, but it is not essential and, indeed, may be omitted.

The semi-colon is a most useful stop ; it indicates a stronger pause than the comma and is often necessary unless we are to be content with very short sentences.

(i) I met John in Town ; so I asked him to dinner.

(ii) He saw life in the raw ; he learned much.

In (i) a semi-colon is preferable to a comma before " so ".

In essays, even at General Certificate stage, the use of the comma instead of a full-stop or a semi-colon is a mistake too often seen.

In descriptive passages the semi-colon is useful to preserve unbroken the complete picture with all its detail.   In the following passage commas could not be used for the semi-colons, and full stops would break the continuity of the scene :

Five-and-thirty years ago the glory had not yet departed from the old coach-roads ; the great roadside inns were still brilliant with well-polished tankards, the smiling glances of pretty barmaids, and the repartees of jocular ostlers ; the mail still announced itself by the merry notes of the horn ; the hedge-cutter or the rick-thatcher might still know the exact hour by the unfailing yet otherwise meteoric apparition of the pea-green Tally-ho or the yellow Independent ; and elderly gentlemen in pony-chaises, quartering nervously to make way for the rolling, swinging swiftness, had not ceased to remark that times were finely changed since they used to see the pack-horses and hear the tinkling of their bells on this very highway.

Felix Holt : GEORGE ELIOT

The colon is now rarely used, except

(i) to introduce a list. Often the colon is followed by a dash.
e.g. The guests included :
Sir James and Lady Hemsley, Mr. and Mrs. T. Hammerston, the Rev. G. O. and Mrs. Ames.
The English table tennis team to meet Scotland at Carlisle on Jan. 13th is :
B. Casofsky, K. Stanley, B. Kennedy, A. Shepherd, Miss A. Wood, Miss B. Steventon.

(ii) to introduce a quotation.
In thinking of Cleopatra we always remember the words of Enobarbus :
" Age cannot wither her, nor custom stale Her infinite variety."

PUNCTUATION EXERCISES

1.—Punctuate the following passage, inserting all necessary capitals :—
The deer on the other hand seemed to enjoy the soft still night air high up upon the mappin terraces the antelopes strode with dignity their shadows flung sharply against the rock as they moved they stood there sharp cut as the animals in noahs ark and around them the night spread wide giving to the encircling shape of regents park the immensities of wide prairies and uncharted forests.

LONDON

2.—Set out the following in the form of a letter with the necessary punctuation and capitals : 23 edward st london ec2 march 8th 1929 messrs day and lee 4 london

road brigham on sea dear sirs we recently sent you as
you had requested a prospectus of waltons modern
business methods and we are hoping to hear that if you
have not already purchased a copy you will order one
now may we again point out that with this book available there is no office problem that cannot be solved it
summarises mens knowledge and experience its authority
is unquestioned its utility is testified to by its readers
see p 21 and it can be bought for 65s we remain dear sirs
yours faithfully brown and co ltd.

J.M.B.

3.—Punctuate and set out the following passage correctly,
inserting all necessary capitals :—
about this time the rev mr. john hussey who had been
some time in trade and was then a clergyman of the
church of england being about to undertake a journey
to aleppo and other parts of the east which he afterwards
accomplished dr johnson who had long been in habits of
intimacy with him honoured him with the following
letter december 29 1778 dear sir i have sent you the
grammar and have left you two books more by which i
hope to be remembered write my name in them we may
perhaps see each other no more you part with my good
wishes nor do i despair of seeing you return let no
opportunities of vice corrupt you let no bad example
seduce you let the blindness of mahometans confirm you
in christianity god bless you i am sir your affectionate
humble servant sam johnson boswells life of johnson.

LONDON

4.—

(a) Punctuate and set out the following passage, inserting
all necessary capitals :—
whos there said mr pickwick starting up in bed boots
sir what do you want please sir can you tell me which
gentleman of your party wears a bright blue dress coat
with a gilt button with pc on it its been given out to
brush thought mr pickwick and the man has forgotten

who it belongs to mr winkle he called out next room
but two on the right hand thankee sir said the boots
and away he went.

(b) Change the punctuation of each of the following sentences so as to give one other meaning, and point out
the difference in meaning produced by the change in
punctuation :—

(i) On joining the Army, he had to obey orders which must
have been irksome to him.

(ii) Few students, I knew, would agree with him.

LONDON

5.—

(a) Rewrite the following in more connected form, with
correct punctuation :—
" Heads, heads—take care of your heads," cried the
loquacious stranger.   " Terrible place—dangerous—
other day—five children—mother—tall lady—eating
sandwiches—forgot the arch—crash—knock—children
look round—mother's head off—sandwich in her
hand—no mouth to put it in."

(b) Change the punctuation of each of the following sentences so as to give one other meaning, and point out
the differences in meaning produced by the change in
punctuation :—

(i) The heckler said the chairman should keep his mouth
shut.

(ii) When did you arrange to meet him on Saturday
evening ?

LONDON

6.—Punctuate, supply the necessary capitals, and paragraph
the following passage :—
A lady from england staying with some friends in
ireland thought to try her hand on the natives of
limerick in the cause of temperance furnished with a
list of names she proceeded to the poorer suburbs
where she called on a mrs doherty good morning mrs
doherty she said in a coaxing tone good morning maam

replied the woman of the house taking her arms out
of the washing tub what can i be doing for you im
collecting for a drunkards home mrs doherty said the
visitor you are maam replied the other then if you send
round about ten oclock to night you can collect
doherty

LONDON

7.—Punctuate the following passage :

the doctor shook his head it was all he could do under
the circumstances and he did it well what sort of night
he said restless sir said mrs harris talk much middling
sir said mrs harris nothing to the purpose I suppose oh
bless you no sir only jargon well said the doctor we
must keep him quiet give him his draughts regularly
and see that he is carefully looked after thats all so
long as mrs jackson and me waits on him no fear of
that said mrs harris

DURHAM

8.—Introduce the necessary capitals and punctuation marks
in the following :—

the twenty-fourth annual meeting of the fairey
aviation company was held on november 13 at 24
bruton street london w sir richard fairey m b e chairman and managing director presided and in the course
of the speech said our factories are busily engaged in
the production of our new naval anti submarine
aircraft the gannet.

R.S.A.

9.—Set out the following passage correctly, inserting all
necessary punctuation marks and re-arranging the
material as you think best :—

the north western office furnishing company ltd
mersey house manchester 15th april 1954 brown and
white worsted spinners union mills bradfield dear sirs
thank you for your order for two typists desks type
4d and two swivel chairs unless there are unforeseen
delays in the supply of timber the equipment will be
delivered by british road services in about three weeks

time yours faithfully per pro the north western office furnishing company ltd t m watson director.

W.R.C.C.

10.—Write out the following passage with correct punctuation, capital letters, and paragraphs :

as i looked over the side of the ship I saw a man floating in the phosphorescent water whats the matter I asked cramp said a voice from an upturned face are you alone on deck yes do you think your captains turned in im sure he isnt i replied could you call him out quietly i am the captain by jove he muttered youre a good swimmer I said you must have come from that ship over there yes ive been in the water since nine oclock may I come aboard.

J.M.B.

Part Five: *FIGURES OF SPEECH*

AN understanding and appreciation of the value of figurative language, or imagery, is most important in the study of English Language and Literature ; yet it is of this that most pupils are ignorant or very vague.

The surprising thing about metaphor and simile is that they are so common in everyday speech that we use and understand them without realising that they are figures of speech.

If your father comes in from work and warns you to be careful, because " the road's like glass," he is using a simile by which in imagination you see the slippery road smooth and like a sheet of glass, and prepare for it.

It is a mistake to think, as some pupils do, that figures of speech are mere devices a poet uses to make his poem more difficult. On the contrary, G. K. Chesterton said : " Keats never put into a sonnet so many remote metaphors as a coster puts into a curse." For example, a coster addresses his friend as " old cock-sparrow," and threatens his opponent that he will " knock his block off." He is speaking figuratively, using the language of pictures. He imagines his opponent's head as a block of wood to be easily knocked off his shoulders. In the same figurative way children call each other " silly ass," " clumsy elephant," or " clever cat," a mother calls her baby " my little chicken" ; later the baby has grown up to be " you little monkey ! " ; a lover calls his girl " honey." Many of our Christian names were originally metaphors ; e.g. flower-names : Rose, Violet, Iris, or gem-names : Ruby, Pearl.

By the use of figures of speech we enlarge our vocabulary and make our speech and writing more vivid and interesting. We may feel, literally, the sun's ray ; but we may also speak, figuratively of a ray of hope ; similarly we literally clean our teeth, but we do not clean the " teeth of a gale."

The Simile (Latin Similis = like) is the expression of a likeness between two *unlike* things.

e.g. The boy ran like the wind. " The boy " and " the wind " are quite different things, compared in the quality of speed.

Note. The two things compared must be different.

If we say—Elsie is like her sister—we have made a comparison, but not a simile. If we say—Elsie is like a tender plant—we have made a simile.

The main purpose of the simile is to make clear what was unknown, by reference to, or likening it to, the known.

We know what a tender plant is like ; it is young and needs careful treatment ; therefore we learn that Elsie is that sort of girl.

Examples of Similes :

Similes :

He is as pleased as a dog with two tails.

He is as straight as the backbone of a herring. (Manx.)

I will wipe Jerusalem as a man wipeth a dish, wiping it, and turning it upside down. (II Kings 21 : 13.)

I wandered lonely as a cloud. (Wordsworth.)

The Assyrian came down like a wolf on the fold. (Byron.)

The Sustained (or Epic) Simile.

The likeness in a simile is generally limited to one or two points of resemblance ; but sometimes a simile is kept up until we have a picture fully drawn—a sustained simile. As these are found in the Epic poetry of Homer, Virgil and Milton, they are sometimes called Epic Similes. e.g.

As when the potent rod
Of Amram's son, in Egypt's evil day,
Waved round the coast, up called the pitchy cloud
Of locusts, warping on the eastern wind,
That o'er the realm of impious Pharaoh hung
Like night, and darkened all the land of Nile ;
So numberless were those bad angels seen
Hovering on wing under the cope of Hell.

Paradise Lost : MILTON

But as a troop of pedlars, from Cabool,
Cross underneath the Indian Caucasus,
That vast sky-neighbouring mountain of milk snow
Crossing so high, that as they mount, they pass
Long flocks of travelling birds dead on the snow
Choked by the air, and scarce can they themselves
Slake their parch'd throats with sugar'd mulberries—
In single file they move, and stop their breath,
For fear they should dislodge the o'erhanging snows—
So the pale Persians held their breath with fear.

(*Sohrab and Rustum* : ARNOLD)

The Metaphor may be termed a compressed simile ; instead of saying a thing is like another, we say a thing *is* another thing. e.g.

Ye are the salt of the earth.
The camel is the ship of the desert.
He is a dog in a manger.
Poor man ! I know he would not be a wolf
But that he sees the Romans are but sheep.

You will find that Psalm 23 is a sustained metaphor.

Often when we feel strongly, the imagination works so quickly that it omits the " like " or " as," which are supplied by the reader, generally unconsciously, in understanding the metaphor. Words are used metaphorically so much in ordinary speech that we scarcely realise that they are metaphors.
e.g. The key to the problem. Just as a key opens a door and allows us to enter, so the key to the problem enables us to open, or understand, and thus to solve the problem. This is " explaining the metaphor," often asked for in examination questions.

Avoid **Mixed Metaphors,** that is, using two different metaphors at the same time.
e.g. The delegate spoke of those who fished in troubled waters, using stacked cards to screen their enmity.

Personification is a figure of speech in which we give human feelings to inanimate objects or abstract ideas. When we speak of a ship as " she " we are giving the ship personality ;

so, too, when we speak of " an angry sea," " a threatening sky."

There is much personification in poetry.

e.g.   Sport that wrinkled Care derides,

     And Laughter holding both his sides.

L'Allegro : MILTON

Metonymy (literally " change of name,"). We gain vividness by substituting a word associated with the thing for the thing itself.

We speak of " grey hairs " when we mean " old age." We read Shakespeare (for his works). Headlines declare " Collapse of England " (English cricketers).

Other examples are :—Put the baby on the bottle (milk) ; from the cradle to the grave (childhood to death) ; the knife (surgery) ; the scaffold (execution).

Synechdoche is a figure of speech in which

 (a) a part is taken for the whole

   e.g. all hands on deck (sailors) ; a sail ! (ship) ; a thousand head of cattle. He has seen seventy winters.

 (b) an individual becomes a class

   e.g. " You play with any Tom, Dick or Harry ! " ; a mother will thus scold her son.

In Gray's " Elegy " we read of " some village Hampden," " some inglorious Milton," " some Cromwell " (referring to men who might have been like Hampden, Milton or Cromwell).

Hyperbole is a figure of speech in which exaggeration is used, not to deceive, but to emphasise. Eastern peoples are prone to such flowery phrases ; in the Bible we find

    " O King, live for ever."

" I will multiply thy seed as the stars of the heaven, and as the sand which is upon the sea shore."

" The hairs of your head are all numbered."

We find this figure of speech often in slang and colloquial English.

e.g. " thousands " for " many " ; " marvellous " for " very good " ; " mad " for " angry." Some sports-writers are guilty of this exaggeration. A missed penalty becomes " a tragic miss " ; and three or four quick wickets in a Test Match are termed " England collapse ". Hyperbole is properly used in such phrases as ; " as old as the hills ", " as quick as lightning ", " it seemed ages ".

Litotes, the opposite of Hyperbole, is an understatement. Sometimes we deny the opposite :

e.g.   He is no fool.

Paul was a citizen of no mean city.

It is not uncommon.

In slang we find " not bad " for " good " ; " rather ! " for an emphatic " yes ", and the curious " not half I didn't ! " for " I did ".

Antithesis is a figure of speech in which two opposite ideas are brought close together in *contrast.* This is often found in proverbial sayings.   e.g.

Man proposes : God disposes.

Speech is silver : silence is golden.

God made the country and man made the town.

Prosperity doth best discover vice, but adversity doth best discover virtue. (BACON)

Better fifty years of Europe than a cycle of Cathay. (TENNYSON)

An Epigram is a short witty saying, which often depends on antithesis for its point.

e.g. This is said to have been written of Charles II in his lifetime :

Here lies a king whose word no man relies on ;

Who never said a foolish thing, and never did a wise one.

Charles replied with another epigram :

True ; my words are my own ; my actions, my ministers'.

Every man desires to live long ; but no man would be old. (SWIFT)

Know then thyself, presume not God to scan.

The proper study of mankind is man. (POPE)

The parson knows enough who knows a duke. (COWPER)

Many epigrams contain a paradox.

A Paradox is a saying which seems to contradict itself ; its seeming nonsense, however, emphasises a truth.

e.g.   Attack is the best form of defence.

More haste less speed.

The child is father of the man. (WORDSWORTH)

Whatever is worth doing at all is worth doing badly.

(G. K. CHESTERTON)

Oxymoron is a kind of condensed paradox. Often the adjective seems to contradict the noun. e.g.

He is condemned to a living death.

There is method in his madness,

I must be cruel, only to be kind. (SHAKESPEARE)

Milton describes gold as " the precious bane " ; and speaks of Hell as a place where there was " no light, but darkness visible."

A Pun is a play upon words, either on two meanings of the same word, or on words sounding alike.

In Shakespeare's day a pun was reputable evidence of agility of mind. Shakespeare uses it often ; sometimes at highly dramatic moments.

e.g.   Gratiano rebukes Shylock :

" Not on thy sole, but on thy soul, harsh Jew,

Thou mak'st thy knife keen."

Lady Macbeth says :

" I'll gild the faces of the grooms withal ;

For it must seem their guilt."

Later the pun was confined to humorous writings and the greatest punster of all was Thomas Hood whose " Faithless Sally Brown " is well known. Here is the last stanza :

" His death, which happened in his berth,

At forty-odd befell :

They went and told the sexton, and

The sexton tolled the bell."

More modern puns :

My husband is at death's door.

The doctor hopes to pull him through.

Is life worth living ? That depends upon the liver.

The pun is sometimes found in advertising slogans :
e.g.   My Goodness. My Guinness.

Climax (literally " a ladder ") is a series of statements in
gradually increasing order of importance.
e.g.   I came, I saw, I conquered.
> Some books are to be tasted, others swallowed, and
> some few to be chewed and digested. (BACON)

Anti-Climax or **Bathos,** the converse of Climax, is a ludi-
crous descent from the sublime to the ridiculous.
The last lines of Tennyson's " Enoch Arden " are bathos :
> " So passed the strong heroic soul away ;
> And when they buried him, the little port
> Had seldom seen a costlier funeral."

Kinglake in " Eothen " uses anti-climax effectively :
Shereef trusted " in the goodness of God, the clenching
power of fate, and the good star of the Englishman."

Euphemism (literally " speak well ") is defined as " a
pleasant way of describing an unpleasant truth."
e.g.   He *passed away*. (He died)
> " He that's coming must be *provided for*. (murdered)
> You are telling *fairy tales*. (lies)

EXERCISES

1.—We speak of " the foot of a tree, a table, a mountain."
Use these metaphorically :—head, nose, neck, mouth,
teeth, jaws, eye, limb, arm, heart.

2.—Colour metaphors.   Give the meaning of :
red tape ; red-letter day ; blue blood ; blue-stocking ;
a bolt from the blue ; white flag ; white feather ; white
lie ; golden mean ; blue moon.

3.—Animal metaphors : Give the meaning of :
cat's paw ; lion's share ; a pig in a poke ; on the high
horse ; swan song ; crocodile tears ; a wolf in sheep's
clothing ; to break the butterfly on the wheel ; to
play ducks and drakes ; a mare's nest.

EXERCISES 53

4.—Here are some Biblical metaphors. Give the meaning, and
    explain the Biblical reference. Use each one in a sentence.
  (a) Job's comforter (Job Ch. 4 to 12) ; a Jonah (Jon. Ch.
      1) ; a prodigal (Luke 15) ; a whited sepulchre (Matt.
      23 : 27 ; a Judas (Matt. 26 : 14) ; a Jehu (2 Kings
      9 : 20) ; a jeremiad (Jer. 51 : 60) ; spoil the Egyp-
      tians (Ex. 3 : 22) ; the writing on the wall (Dan. 5 :
      25-28) ; a scapegoat (Lev. 16 : 10).
  (b) a shibboleth (Judges 12 : 6) ; the old Adam ; a
      daughter of Eve ; a son of Belial (I Sam. 2 : 12) ;
      an apocryphal statement ; the law of the Medes and
      Persians (Dan. 6 : 8) ; to rob Peter to pay Paul ;
      out-Herod Herod (Matt. 2 : 16) ; the curse of Cain
      (Gen. 4 : 11) ; a broken reed (2 Kings 18 : 21).

5.—Classical metaphors : Give the meaning and explain
    the classical reference. Use each one in a sentence.
    Cross the Rubicon ; Fabian tactics ; Stygian gloom ;
    the Gordian knot ; the sword of Damocles ; a Pyrrhic
    victory ; a Parthian shot ; a modern Croesus ; a
    Philippic ; the Achilles heel.

6.—Give the origin and meaning of six of the following
    metaphorical expressions, and introduce them into six
    sentences :
    to throw up the sponge ; a bolt from the blue ; to
    bell the cat ; to play to the gallery ; to draw in one's
    horns ; to take pot-luck ; to eat humble pie ; to take
    a firm stand.

LONDON

7.—Select THREE of the following sentences, and explain the
    meaning of each, showing why the metaphor contained
    in it suggests such a meaning.
  (a)
   (i) Our guesses were very wide of the mark.
  (ii) His mind was clouded with his own conceit.
 (iii) The workers were not allowed to air their grievances.
  (iv) The besieged were at the end of their tether.

(v) Always working against the grain, I followed this unpleasant occupation for several months.

J.M.B.

(b)

(i) For three days and nights our safety hung in the balance.
(ii) His strength was ebbing fast.
(iii) We were disarmed by his friendly manner.
(iv) I have an open mind with regard to the question.
(v) His speech was full of veiled threats.

J.M.B.

8.—

(a) Use **Four** of the following expressions, each in a separate
sentence, so as to show quite clearly that you understand their meaning :

to beat about the bush ; to strike while the iron is hot ;
to cut one's coat according to one's cloth ; to make both
ends meet ; to turn the tables on ; to burn the midnight oil.

(b) Write sentences, **One** for each word chosen, using *five*
of the following words in a *metaphorical* sense :—

hinge, cloud, flood, iron (adjective), thirst, wreck, fruit,
crown.   LONDON

9.—Explain the metaphors contained in **Four** of the following
sentences :

(i) The car flashed past us at sixty miles an hour.
(ii) His generous bequests will keep his memory green.
(iii) He is a mine of information.
(iv) The evidence heard gave some colour to his accusations.
(v) I could not get a word in edgeways.
(vi) He awaited the result with great anxiety, for his whole
future was at stake.

J.M.B.

10.—From the list of **Twelve** idioms supplied below, select the
Ten correct ones to fill the blank space in the following
sentences :

(i) When the harm is done it's no use . . . . . . , though some
optimists hold that . . . . . .

(ii) In these days of rationing . . . . . . , and the bill of fare usually offers little but . . . . . .

(iii) ' Thompson ' is of course only his . . . . . . : modesty has always made him . . . . . .

(iv) You must . . . . . . and not . . . . . . because this affair is still a secret.

(v) He is a . . . . . . and foreigners make him . . . . . .
(1) a regular John Bull ; (2) mind your p's and q's ; (3) nom de plume ; (4) see red ; (5) gild the lily ; (6) hide his light under a bushel ; (7) crying over split milk ; (8) enough is as good as a feast ; (9) it's never too late to mend ; (10) Hobson's choice ; (11) let the cat out of the bag ; (12) Parthian shot.

OXFORD AND CAMBRIDGE

11.—Express in your own words the literal meaning of the following figurative passages.

(i)   Sceptre and crown
Must tumble down,
And in the dust be equal made
With the poor crooked scythe and spade.

(ii) Nature, a mother kind alike to all,
Still grants her bliss at labour's earnest call.

(iii)   The sea of fortune doth not ever flow,
She draws her favours to the lowest ebb :
Her tides have equal times to come and go ;
Her loom doth weave the fine and coarsest web.

J.M.B.

12.—Choose **Four** of the following words and write **Four** sentences each containing one of the words used metaphorically and clearly bringing out its meaning :
thread, start, storm, core, hinge, stronghold.   J.M.B.

13.—Do the same with **Four** of these :
(a) rod, anchor, plough, hand, bridge, tower.
(b) heart, herald, sword, cloak, rock, whitewash (verb).

14.—Add a suitable noun to these adjectives and explain the phrase :

Homeric, Shavian, Herculean, Parthian, quixotic, stoic, spartan, Machiavellian, Pecksniffian, Falstaffian.

15.—Give, with reasons, your opinion as to the appropriateness of the metaphor.

(a) Mussolini was the architect of his country's ruin.

(b) Mary, with her placid temperament, was a veritable thermometer in regulating the feverish enthusiasms of her friend.

(c) The choir never put a foot wrong.

16.—Use these metaphorical expressions in sentences to show that you understand their meaning :
an eyesore ; a firebrand ; a windfall ; throw cold water on ; to ring the changes ; read between the lines ; a flash in the pan ; on the wane ; throw up the sponge ; pay the piper.

17.—Give the meaning of each of the following without using obvious metaphors :

(i) The professor is a mine of information.

(ii) It would be pleasant if we could import unlimited food-stuffs, but we must cut our coat according to the cloth.

(iii) He was such a turncoat that you could never believe in the sincerity of his political declarations.

(iv) He persisted in burning the candle at both ends until he fell seriously ill.

(v) I wanted to carry out a thorough investigation of the transactions, but my partner advised me to let sleeping dogs lie.

(vi) When John had fired us with enthusiasm for his project, Jim came along and threw cold water on all our plans.

J.M.B.

18.—Explain the metaphors contained in **Three** of the following sentences :

(i) In the crisis, he proved a man of straw.

(ii) His only hope of advancement was by stepping into his father's shoes.

(iii) He decided to pocket the insult and withdraw.
(iv) On the matter of our economic recovery, he confessed we were not yet out of the wood.
 (v) As a young barrister, he won his spurs in the criminal court.

DURHAM

19.—Name the figures of speech in each of the following sentences and give the meaning of each sentence in your own words.
(a) His talk was a perpetual feast.
(b) I led that boy a dog's life.
(c) All the perfumes of Arabia will not sweeten this little hand.
(d) Thy word is a lamp unto my feet and a light unto my path.
(e) Chance is blind.
(f) Give every man thine ear, but few thy voice.
(g) And, like a dam, the mighty wreck lay right athwart the stream.
(h) He was playing to the gallery.
(i) He looked as though his face had been cut out of marble with a blunt chisel.
(f) Heaven's air is better than the cold, dead grave.

20.—
(a) Choose **Four** of the following metaphorical expressions. Give the meaning of each and suggest circumstances in which each might be used :
(i) read between the lines ; (ii) working in the dark ; (iii) a catspaw ; (iv) to be wise after the event ; (v) face the music ; (vi) ride rough-shod over ; (vii) beat about the bush ; (viii) putting the clock back.
(b) Choose **Three** of the following words, and show how each can be used as a metaphor by including it in a sentence of your own composition :
veil, harvest, poison, path, smile.

LONDON

C

Part Six: COMPOSITION

JOINING SENTENCES

1.—Combine each pair of statements in one sentence.
 (a) by using a conjunction or relative pronoun.
 (b) by changing a verb into a noun.
e.g. She failed in the examination. We were disappointed.
 (a) We were disappointed when she failed in the examination.
 (b) Her failure in the examination disappointed us.

 (1) The umpires appeared. The crowd applauded.

 (2) I offered him my subscription. He gratefully accepted it.

 (3) There was an announcement in the evening paper. Mr. Harris was dead.

 (4) It is raining heavily. We shall go out.

 (5) He failed many times. He succeeded at last.

 (6) The man was arrested. He had stolen a watch.

 (7) We were very angry. Joan refused to keep us.

 (8) Our team lost the match. The centre-forward was not there.

 (9) We thanked John. John had invited us to a party.

 (10) The gangster threatened us. We laughed.

2.—Join these sentences in three different ways :
 (a) My brother came to see me. He asked for my help.
 (b) John went for a walk. He wore his new coat.
 (c) We waited at the corner for a bus. The bus was late.
 (d) At the wedding there were many guests. They brought gifts.
 (e) He hit the ball hard. He was caught.

(f) The district has many coal mines. There is lovely country near.

(g) The weather has been treacherous. The farmers have gathered the harvest.

(h) He returned my book. He had not read it.

(i) I receive pocket-money. This is soon spent.

(j) My sister is fat. My sister is jolly.

3.—Join these sentences into one sentence, varying the joining words as much as possible.

(a) Tom was a new boy. He was in Form IIc. Tom felt strange in his new school. He was very unhappy. Tom soon made friends. One of his friends was called Dick. The name of the other was Harry.

(b) York is a city. York stands on the River Ouse. York was famous in Roman times. York has a Minster. The mediaeval walls of York still stand.

(c) We kicked off. The ball was passed from wing to wing. We swept down the field. Our centre-forward received the ball. He was in the penalty area. He scored.

(d) The Governors called in experts. The experts gave advice. The field should be re-sown. Parts of the field had been worn bare. These were near the goal-posts.

(e) We spent a long day at the seaside. We went to Ramsgate. We went in the car. We sat on the sands. We ate ice-cream. The weather was glorious.

(f) Some Latin verbs were set for homework. John learnt his homework. Next morning the master asked him to repeat them. John could not. He had forgotten every word.

4.—

(i) Combine the following simple sentences so as to form **one** complex sentence :

The river was much swollen after the heavy rain. The rain had fallen incessantly for two days and nights. The river threatened to wash away the old bridge. Many of the men living in the suburbs went to work over this bridge.

(ii) Combine the following sentences in **three** ways as different from one another as possible :

The writing was very faded. I couldn't make out the signature.

(iii) Compose three sentences each conveying the main idea of the following sentence, but each securing emphasis of one of the italicised words :

Mary went alone by *air* to Paris *last* April. J.M.B.

5.—Rewrite the following in connected form, using only two sentences :—

He was returning home across the park. He had been taking two hours' brisk exercise. He was returning in the dusk. His foot struck against a stump. The stump was hidden. He fell flat. He was up again in an instant. He said, " There is no damage except to the knees of my trousers." The party looked anxiously at each other. They remembered the death of Lord Lansdowne. They regretted his death. They were not quite at ease till next morning. Then he joined the breakfast table with unshaken spirits. He had his usual buoyancy of step.

LONDON

DESCRIPTIONS

A. SHARPENING A SCYTHE.

There is an art in the sharpening of a scythe, and it is worth describing carefully. Your blade must be dry, and that is why you will see men rubbing the scythe-blade with grass before they whet it. Then also your rubber must be quite dry, and on this account it is a good thing to lay it on your coat and keep it there during all your day's mowing. The scythe you stand upright, with the blade pointing away from you, and you put your left hand firmly on the back of the blade, grasping it ; then you pass the rubber first down one side of the blade-edge and then down the other, beginning near the handle and going on to the point and working quickly and hard. When you first do this you will, perhaps, cut your hand ; but it is only at first that such an accident will happen to you.

To tell when the scythe is sharp enough this is the rule. First the stone clangs and grinds against the iron harshly ; then it rings musically to one note ; then, at last, it purrs as though the iron and stone were exactly suited. When you hear this, your scythe is sharp enough ; and I, when I heard it that June dawn, with everything quite silent except the birds, let down the scythe and bent myself to mow.

(from *Hills and the Sea* : HILAIRE BELLOC)

In this passage you will notice some of the qualities of good descriptive writing.

(i) There is keen observation : he has seen it done and done it himself.

(ii) There is an orderliness about it—from the preparation of the scythe before whetting to the time it is ready for the mowing.

(iii) It is simple in style. The words are easy to understand ; yet they are the exact words to use (The French have a phrase " le mot juste ".) e.g. purrs, whet, clang.

(iv) It is intimate. It speaks of " you " and " I " as though he is teaching you, and you have the job to do.

(v) It has a good beginning and a good ending.

B. THE CIGARETTE-MAKING MACHINE.

The automatic cigarette-making machine, while complicated in appearance and exceedingly ingenious, is fairly simple in principle. Instead of individual cigarette papers, a long roll of cigarette paper of the appropriate width is used, and the first step is to print on the paper the name of the brand. This is done by a machine which works at a regulated rate, so that it makes an impression so many times a second according to the speed at which the " tape " of paper passes under its stamp.

The paper then has the tobacco, cut very fine, placed on it from a funnel. It passes further along, and one edge is folded over the other, the opposite edge having been gummed by another device. At this stage the cigarette is like a long tube of tobacco, and the final stage in manufacture is the cutting into the required length. This is done by a sharp knife which descends at regular intervals. It will readily be seen that in this machine everything is done by timing.

(from Science in Industry : A. M. Low)

Here is a technical description of a machine. This has the same qualities of observation, orderliness and simplicity.

Note how each sentence is linked with the one following : e.g. the last phrase in Sentence I is " fairly simple in principle." Sentence II tells us what the principle is, and leads us on to the " printing ". Sentence III begins " This (the printing) is done ". Just as in the machine itself one process leads on to another, so in the passage there is a smooth orderliness.

You will notice that in this passage there is not the same intimacy as in A. It cannot be as personal because the subject is a machine. Do not think it is any worse as a description. The style is rightly determined by the subject.

Reports are another type of description. These call primarily for a factual description of things as you see them, with perhaps some estimate of causes, and your own opinion or recommendations as a result of your observations.

EXERCISES (Descriptions)

1.—Describe in a paragraph one of these :

  (a) The contents of your pockets—(which you have emptied on to the table).

  (b) The outside of your house.

  (c) Your mother's clothes when she is doing housework.

  (d) Your mother dressed for paying a visit.

  (e) The view from your bedroom window.

2.—Give an account of your first attempt to use a telephone.

3.—Describe **one** of the following, using the words given in as interesting a way as possible, so that they no longer appear as a catalogue.

(a) A *garden* in which grow geraniums, marigolds, roses, lavender, lilies, mignonette, pansies, nasturtiums, water-lilies.

(b) A *sea-beach* where there are rocks, shells, jelly-fish, sea-weed, limpets, crabs, drift-wood, seagulls, sea-foam.

(c) A *town* which has streets, omnibuses, cinemas, a library, churches, hotels, schools, hospitals, shops.

4.—Describe accurately and in not more than fifty words for each, two of the following :

(a) (i) Filling a fountain-pen ; (ii) Some stroke in swimming ; (iii) Dismounting a bicycle ; (iv) A match-box.

(b) (i) Washing one's hands ; (ii) Packing a picnic-basket ; (iii) Making a bonfire in the garden ; (iv) Writing on the blackboard.

LONDON

5.—Describe clearly **One** of the following :

(a) A miner's safety lamp ;

(b) how to repair a punctured bicycle tyre ;

(c) how to lay a fire ;

(d) how to use a chisel ;

(e) how to measure the expansion of a metal rod.

6.—Give a brief description, without sketches, of a barometer, *or* a suspension bridge *or* a brace and bit.

7.—Describe without sketches **One** of these :
a hand camera ; an electric kettle ; how the pedals of a bicycle drive the back wheel.

8.—Give clear and simple directions to housewives on the handling of electrical equipment in the home.

I.C.E. & I.E.E.

9.—Subjects for Paragraphs about people at work or at play.

(a) A joiner making a dovetail joint.

(b) A ballerina practising.

(c) A blacksmith tyreing a wheel.

(d) A bus driver in a fog.

(e) A shot-firer in a coal mine.

(f) A deck-hand on a herring drifter, hauling the nets.

(g) A forward in a rugby scrum near his own line.

(h) A cricketer nearing his century while batting.

(i) A swimmer practising for a high-diving competition.

(j) A potter throwing a vase.

(k) A workman replacing a broken window-pane.

(l) A boy making a kite.

(m) A girl typing her first exercise.

(n) A man painting the outside of a house.

(o) A woman preparing a chicken for the oven.

10.—Choose **One** of the objects mentioned below. Explain in **One** sentence what it is used for. Then write no more than four sentences to explain how it works.
(i) a pair of scissors ; (ii) a safety-pin ; (iii) A fountain-pen ; (iv) a shuttle.

J.M.B.

11.—Attempt **One** of the following :

(a) Describe accurately *in words* a spring balance *or* a vacuum flask *or* an electric iron *or* a telephone kiosk.

(b) Write in connected sentences instructions for inflating and lacing a football, *or* testing and adjusting brakes on a bicycle, *or* making your favourite dish, *or* making a bed.

(c) Draft a notice which would be typed and displayed on your school notice board, announcing (with reasons) that, until further notice, the main entrance to the building will be closed during the dinner break. Students are to use the side entrances, one for either sex.

A.E.B. (*Specimen Paper*)

12.—Explain, with sketches if necessary, the working principle of :
  (a) a shock absorber ; (b) a household tap ; (c) an electric bell ; (d) a potter's wheel ; (e) a gear box ; (f) a pendulum clock ; (g) a doctor's thermometer.

13.—For the benefit of a friend describe the preparation and take-off of an aircraft, *or* how a motor-cycle is propelled.

14.—Describe simply how at least two fundamental mechanical laws are made use of in an ordinary pedal bicycle.

I.C.E. & I.E.E.

EXERCISES (Reports)

1.—You were a witness of an accident which took place on a Zebra Crossing. Write a report of the accident for use by the police.

2.—Write a report for an Insurance Company on an accident which has taken place on a lathe in the workshop, resulting in the crushing of the operator's hand.

3.—Your firm is considering a new machine to replace one that is proving uneconomical in use. You have been sent to witness a demonstration of this new machine. Submit your report as to its suitability for the purpose required.

4.—Write a report on the damage caused by a recent fire in your works, and make recommendations.

5.—You have been sent to examine a large building which your company proposes to take over and adapt. Write a report on its present condition and state your recommendations.

I.C.E. & I.E.E.

PAIRS

Each of the following pairs of words indicates two substances, articles or ideas having something in common, yet differing in one respect.

c*

In each case say what the words have in common and explain the difference between them.

(i) A strike and a lock-out ; discovery and invention ; a Bill and an Act of Parliament ; the House of Commons and the House of Lords ; analysis and synthesis.

(ii) Translucent and opaque ; malleable and ductile ; circumference and perimeter ; level and perpendicular ; elastic and plastic.

(iii) Brazing and welding ; kinetic energy and potential energy ; hardening and tempering ; coke and coal ; a motor and a dynamo.

(iv) Oil and grease ; central heating and open fire ; a watch and a pendulum clock ; a microphone and a loudspeaker ; liquid and gas.

(v) A Spitfire and a Comet ; a balloon and a dirigible ; a hacksaw and a tenon-saw ; a chisel and a gouge ; a petrol engine and a diesel engine.

WHY ?

Write paragraphs to explain :—

1.—Why is it easier to float in the Dead Sea than in the Mediterranean ?

2.—Why does washing in hard water need more soap than in soft water ?

3.—Why did Alcock and Brown fly from America to Europe rather than Europe to America ?

4.—Why is it difficult to spear an object lying at the bottom of a pool ?

5.—Why is a house without a damp-course liable to have damp walls when the ground is wet ?

6.—How do the grooves on a gramophone record become sounds ?

7.—Why do we electro-plate the exposed parts of a motor car ?

8.—Why can we lift a heavy load with a hydraulic jack ?

9.—Why do water pipes burst in winter ?

10.—Why is a thermos flask a good place to keep ice cream ?

11.—Why do Comet planes fly at 40,000 feet ?

12.—Why have modern cars adopted the present shapes ?

COLLOQUIALISMS

" Reading maketh a full man, conference a ready man, and writing an exact man."

(BACON)

When we talk to our friends we use words more loosely than we should when we write. We often speak disjointedly or use vague phrases and repetitions when we cannot think of the right word. These colloquialisms are permissible in ordinary conversation but not in writing, which " maketh an exact man."

It is true that correct speech helps correct writing but not all speak well ; and the following exercises are given to check the faults of those who put down on paper words and phrases just as they come into their minds, as if they were continuing a conversation.

EXERCISE

Re-write these sentences, changing the colloquial words and phrases into clear and exact English.

(a) I've seen that happen no end of times but nobody seems to take any sort of notice.

(b) Did you have a good do last night ? Oh, yes, we didn't half enjoy ourselves.

(c) I didn't think much of the picture last night ; did you ?

(d) I think I'd better do a bit of work tonight or I shall be for it in the morning.

(e) A garden takes a lot of looking after.

(f) I'm not bothered whether I go or not.

(g) I've seen him somewhere or other.

(h) I thought I'd got a detention but I was let off.

(i) Round our way nobody bothers much about getting dressed up.

(j) He's got a posh new car that must have cost a bit.

(k) Most nights there's nothing much doing in our village.

(l) I've been doing that quite a lot now.

(m) I don't think much of her new dress. Oh, it's not bad. I rather like it.

(n) Somehow or other I can't stick that man.

(o) He has some sort of a job at the Copper Works or somewhere like that.

(p) He spent a long time on making a rockery but it was nothing much at the finish.

(q) We shall get it in the morning because everybody's got the wrong answer.

(r) The bell goes at ten o'clock and then we go to Physics.

(s) The doctor has a boy to do the garden, get the coals in and go errands.

(t) I'll never get done with all this work to do.

DEFINITIONS

Rules

(i) A definition must be **one** sentence.

(ii) It must not include any unnecessary idea, or an idea which is only sometimes true.

(iii) It should say in the simplest words what the thing is, not what it is not.

Examples

(a) A vacuum cleaner is a machine that removes dust by means of suction.

(b) A sculptor is an artist who carves figures.

(c) A balloon is an envelope or bag designed to float in the air when inflated.

(d) A staircase is a structure by means of which ascent or descent may be made, a step at a time, from one level to another.

EXERCISES

1.—Write, in sentence form, brief definitions of three of the
following : (i) Antipodes ; (ii) leading articles ; (iii)
archaeology ; (iv) referendum ; (v) arbitration ; (vi)
afforestation. J.M.B.

2.—Criticise **three** of the following definitions, pointing out
where they are inaccurate and suggesting improvements :—
(a) A church is a building with stained glass windows and
a spire.
(b) Superstition means believing in spirits.
(c) A bicycle is a two-wheeled vehicle propelled by human
energy.
(d) A politician is one who is interested in politics.
DURHAM

3.—Point out as many faults as you can in each of the following definitions :
(i) A table is a wooden square with four legs.
(ii) An argument is when two people argue about something.
J.M.B.

4.—Give brief definitions of **three** of the following :
(i) jubilee ; (ii) glimpse ; (iii) pollution ; (iv) geology ;
(v) horticulture.

5.—Say what is wrong with the following definitions :
(i) A window is an oblong glass part of the wall of a house
that you can see through.
(ii) A wheelbarrow is to take things from one field to another
(iii) A monoplane is an aeroplane with one wing.
Give a correct definition of **One** of the above objects.
J.M.B.

SIMPLIFICATION AND MODERNISATION

1.—Rewrite the following sentences from a newspaper account
of a wedding in good simple English :
(i) The nuptials were solemnized between the happy pair.

(ii) The ceremony was impressively performed by the Rev. J. Smith who ably officiated.

(iii) The organist commenced the service with a charming rendition of Handel's immortal ' Largo.'

(iv) The bride presented a charming appearance, being attired in a classical gown of white satin ; and a bouquet of pink roses was carried.

(v) The best man expressed a wish that their voyage through life together might take them along sunny paths and through flowery groves.

OXFORD AND CAMBRIDGE

2.—Rewrite the following sentences simply and in as few words as possible without loss of meaning.

(i) In the event of his being successful at the polls he has formed the design of holding in the near future a debate open to anyone who wishes to attend on a subject of major importance and of interest to every human being.

(ii) Adverse climatic conditions and the disabilities of physical exhaustion put obstacles in the way of our taking a pedestrian excursion.

(iii) His collaborators were endeavouring to erect their ponderous superstructure without previously taking the precaution to contrive an adequate foundation.

J.M.B.

3.—Rewrite the following sentences in good plain English, avoiding the words in italics.

(a) The *retention* of this *prohibition* will *engender* much *animosity*.

(b) His strength has been *depleted* by his recent *indisposition*, but a holiday should *expedite* his *recuperation*.

(c) His *misdemeanour* is not of serious *magnitude*.

(d) *Centenarians* are *notoriously prone* to boasting of their *longevity*.

(e) My *abhorrence* of the *procedure* was *overridden* by their *incessant importunity* and at last I *reluctantly acquiesced.*

DURHAM

4.—The following words are spoken by an African character in a novel written in the eighteenth century. Write a simplified version (not a summary) of the passage, keeping the ideas in their original order.

In enumerating the particular comforts of life, we shall find many advantages on the side of the Europeans. They cure wounds and diseases with which we languish and perish. We suffer inclemencies of weather which they can obviate. They have engines for the despatch of many laborious works which we must perform by manual industry. And, if we descend to the privacies of life, their habitations are more commodious, and their possessions are more secure.

J.M.B.

5.—Express the following in modern English :—

But indeed the perfect good and honest man should never covet outward glory but as a mean to bring him to noble attempts, whereby he might procure the better credit of his doings. And for a young man that coveteth honour by virtue, give him a little to glory in his well-doing : for as Theophrastus saith, virtue buddeth and flourisheth in youth, and taketh fast root by praises given, as wit and courage groweth in them.

LONDON

REASONING

1.—Point out what is illogical in the following sentences :
  (i) It is a full day's work even to open, much less to acknowledge, all my correspondence.
  (ii) His gift to the hospital is only one of the latest of the many acts of kindness with which he has benefited the town before now.
  (iii) Your teaching must have had and probably has had a stimulating effect on your pupils.

J.M.B.

2.—Comment on the weakness of the argument in each of
   the following passages :

   (i) I saw Mr. X reading the *Daily Worker* in the station
       waiting-room to-day.   I did not know he was a
       Communist.

  (ii) " If you don't take pocket-handkerchiefs and watches,"
       said the Dodger, " then some other cove will : so
       that the cove what loses them will be all the worse
       and you'll be all the worse, too, and nobody half a
       ha'porth the better, except the chaps what gets 'em—
       and you've just as good a right to them as they have."

 (iii) " Mary was one of the cleverest in her school, yet she
       has not gained a scholarship ; that just shows that the
       examination does not pick out the best candidates."

                                                       J.M.B.

STATISTICAL DIAGRAMS AND GRAPHS

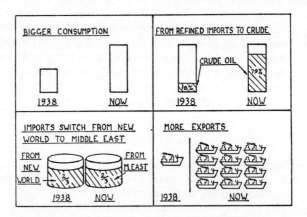

1.—Basing your account on the information given in the
    diagram above, write a short report on " Oil—Changes
    in Britain's position since 1938."

    ASSOCIATED EXAMINATIONS BOARD (*Specimen Paper*)

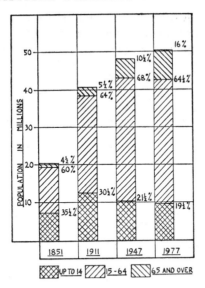

2.—

(a) Briefly state the problem which this diagram illustrates.

(b) Suggest some measures which could be taken to deal
with the problem.

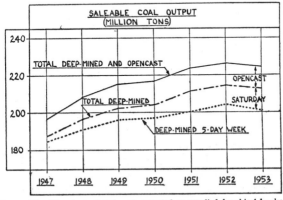

Note. 16·6 million tons of coal were exported or supplied for ships' bunkers.

3.—After studying the chart on the previous page and the note below it, write a reply to a letter from

(a) A man protesting against the spoiling of the countryside by opencast working ; *or*

(b) A miner who objects to working on Saturdays.

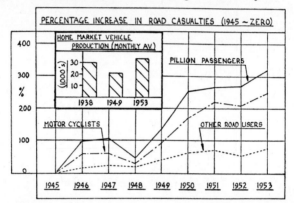

4.—Basing your account on information given in the graph above write a short report on " The Problem of Road Safety."

5.—Supposing you had to compare the relative prosperity of two towns, A and B, what statistics would you try to obtain and what value would they have ?

6.—Discuss the statement " Figures can prove anything."

REPORTED SPEECH

A conversation between a customer and her butcher.

" May I have a little best steak, please ? "

" I am sorry, madam, but I have only chops. I will let you have some steak next week."

Here we have the actual words of the speakers. (Direct Speech.)

This is turned into Reported Speech, or Indirect Speech.

A lady asked her butcher if she might have a little best steak.

The butcher replied that he was sorry but he had only chops. He would let her have some steak in the following week.

From this example you will probably learn how to change Direct to Reported Speech more easily than from a list of rules. A little ingenuity is at times necessary to ensure that the Reported Speech reads smoothly and without ambiguity. You will learn by practice.

EXERCISES

1.—Rewrite the following passage in reported (indirect) speech :

MR. JONES : I feel I cannot resume my seat without referring to tomorrow's meeting, at which the Vicar has promised to be present.

MR. SMITH (interrupting) : Keep to the point !

MR. JONES : In my opinion, I am doing so, for we all know what the Vicar's views are on this subject.

OXFORD AND CAMBRIDGE

2.—Write the following passage, which is in reported speech, in direct speech, giving the exact words used by Columbus :

Colombus then reminded his crew of the orders he had given them on leaving the Canaries, that, after sailing all day, they should not go any farther after midnight. He thought it probable that they would approach land that very night ; he ordered, for that reason, that they should stay where they were for that night, and proceed the following morning.

J.M.B.

3.—The following extract gives, in reported speech and inadequately punctuated, part of a dramatic dialogue. Rewrite it, punctuating it carefully and giving the dialogue as direct speech, in the form of a play, i.e., precede each speech by the speaker's name, and include in the form of stage directions any narrative or descriptive details which cannot be embodied in the dialogue. The Doctor asked Mr. Twigg if he had fixed up about the marquee for the following Wednesday. Mr. Twigg replied that it was to be there that afternoon. They had wanted to send them a black and yellow striped thing but he had said white. The Doctor exclaimed that he should hope so what did they think it was for a school-treat. After a short pause during which he walked about restlessly the Doctor said he wished the Major would be quick. Mr. Twigg asked if that wasn't the Major over there. The Doctor answered in the affirmative. After another pause the Doctor asked what was the general feeling about the Major in the village. Mr. Twigg said of course people realised what a lot the Major did. The Doctor then asked if Mr. Twigg thought the Major did a lot and Mr. Twigg answered hesitatingly in the negative and said that he didn't think the Major did as much as the Doctor did. The Doctor asked if the young men supported the Major and Mr. Twigg replied that they did. For instance the Major was always going down to the club playing billiards and reminding the young men that he had presented the new billiard balls but never mentioned that the Doctor had presented the table. The Doctor supposed they didn't know he had raised the money to found the club. Mr. Twigg said he was sure they didn't because he hadn't known it either. The Doctor never let people know what he did for them. The Doctor asked Mr. Twigg indignantly if he thought he was the sort of man to do that and Mr. Twigg said that when all was said and done the young men could hardly be expected to know unless they were told.

J.M.B.

4.—Rewrite the following passage in direct speech, i.e. giving the actual words used by the speakers. Pay great attention to punctuation and paragraphing.

Brown asked him which train he intended catching, and

Smith replied that he hoped to get the 4-30. It would arrive in London in time for him to reach home before dark. Brown wished he were accompanying Smith, for he had not been to London that year. He would be going in December, but he much preferred the summer. He asked Smith how long he had lived in London, and on Smith's replying that he had lived there ten years, Brown exclaimed in surprise that it was remarkable how quickly time passed. It seemed only the previous day that they had been boys at school together.

                                                                J.M.B.

LETTERS

The G.P.O. delivers, on an average, thirty million letters, postcards and parcels every week-day. Many of these are personal letters, and the way in which they are written concerns no one but the sender and the recipient. Even so, such letters should be written with care, for we should hardly wish our friends to think that we could not spell or punctuate.

Some letters, however, are very important, for in them we introduce ourselves to the general public, or to a possible employer. Every club or society needs a secretary, an officer with responsibility and some prestige, who must be able to write letters worthy of his organization and the place he holds in it.

Letters should be written on good note-paper with an envelope to match. They should be brief and to the point, and with no spelling errors or words crossed out. For a long time you may need to write the letter ' in rough ' and then make a ' fair copy.'

You may find the following specimen letters some guidance. Specimens of business letters will be found elsewhere in the book (see Précis No. 21, pp. 120 to 123). It should be noted, however, that the style and lay-out of business letters may vary to some extent from one office to another. Having learnt the fundamentals of letter-writing you must then see what is required in the office where you are employed.

SPECIMEN LETTERS

(1) To the Editor *The Fairley Gazette*.

23 HANSON AVENUE,
FAIRLEY.
30*th October*, 1954.

Dear Sir,

Last week there was another accident at Plough Corner. The problem of this danger-spot has never been tackled, because it has been thought that a costly major operation is necessary, involving the demolition of the old Plough Inn.

I suggest to the local Road Safety Committee that they consider a very simple remedy—to erect at Plough Corner a HALT sign, illuminated at night, for all traffic from Smawthorne.

It may seem illogical to halt this main road traffic rather than that of the minor road to Belshaw, but I think it would be effective.

Yours faithfully,
D. JOHNSON.

(2) From the Secretary of a Society.

23 HANSON AVENUE,
FAIRLEY.
28*th September*, 1954.

Dear Mr. Waters,

The President and Committee of the Fraxonian Society invite you to be their guest at their Annual Dinner at the Black Swan Inn on November 8th at 7-30 p.m.

They would be honoured if you would respond to the toast " Our Visitors."

Yours faithfully,
D. JOHNSON.
(*Hon. Sec.*)

(3) Application in answer to an advertisement.

54 SWEET ST.,
FAIRLEY.
3rd December, 1954.

Messrs. B. HURFORD & CO. LTD.
Dear Sirs,

In answer to your advertisement in today's " Fairley Gazette " for a shorthand-typist, I beg to apply for the post.

I am seventeen years of age and was educated at Fairley Modern School.

For the last two years I have been an assistant in Messrs. Brierley's bookshop in High Street, Dunfield, and have regularly attended evening classes at Dunfield Technical College, in shorthand (100 words a minute), typewriting (60 words a minute) and secretarial practice.

I enclose copies of testimonials from the Headmaster of Fairley Modern School and from my present employer, and I am permitted to refer you to :

(i) The Rev. G. Griffiths, The Manse, Wesley St., Fairley.

(ii) Mr. A. Place, B.Sc., Principal, The Technical College, Dunfield.

Yours faithfully,
DORIS COOMBES.

Letters to Write :

1.—Write a letter to a seaside hotel or boarding-house proprietor, enquiring the necessary details for a proposed holiday visit. Draw and address an envelope for the return letter to yourself.

2.—Write a letter to your General Manager, suggesting reasons for a change in the date of the annual works' holiday.

3.—A boy about to leave school wishes to take up accountancy. Write a letter advising him briefly on the course he must take and the prospects in the profession, *or* Write him a letter tactfully discouraging him from taking up accountancy.

4.—An accident to your assistant leaves you single-handed. Write a letter to your employers reporting the accident, the action you took, and what you propose to do pending their instructions.

5.—Write two short letters.
(i) From a customer to a firm complaining about the inferior quality of an article supplied.
(ii) The firm's reply.

6.—A consignment of perishable goods to your firm has suffered badly during transit on British Railways. Write a letter to British Railways, giving full details and making a claim for the loss.

7.—Advertisements to answer.
(a) The Warbrick Food Machinery Engineering Co. Ltd. have an immediate vacancy in their drawing-office at Swanley Hall for a JUNIOR DETAIL DRAUGHTSMAN. Write giving full details, education, training and experience to the Secretary, Swanley Hall, Swanley.
(b) Lady Shorthand Typist wanted, with clerical experience, for wool firm : state age, experience, salary required. Reply Brown Bros. Ltd., Scotton Buildings, Bratley.

8.—Write two short letters.
(i) To a firm complaining about the delay in repairing your television set.
(ii) The firm's reply.

9.—Write an indignant letter to your local newspaper, about the noise made in the road where you live by people returning from dances after midnight.

10.—Write a letter inviting a speaker to address a club of which you are secretary.

11.—As secretary of a club, write a letter of sympathy to a member on the death of his son.

12.—The following message was left for his Secretary by Mr. O. T. Smith, General Manager.

Assume that you are the Secretary and write the appropriate letter :

MEMO :	HOWARD & GROVES, LTD., MARKET HOUSE, TADWORSTER, YORKS.
Miss Brown	Pl write Oldroyd & Jenkins and thank for excellent arrangements for staff outing. Ask quotation for private dinner party—Ackerley Village Hall, Friday 27 Feb. start 7-30. 18 people, four course, if possible turkey. All furniture there but caterers to provide table ware and linen, floral decorations etc. also entertainment—if so, terms. Their address :— 16 Market St., Heckcaster. O.T.S.

W.R.C.C.

13.—Write telegrams dealing with **Two** of the following sets of circumstances :
  (a) As secretary of a football club you wish to cancel a match as the ground is unfit.
  (b) You wish to reserve accommodation at an hotel for tonight and tomorrow night.
  (c) You wish to obtain a new piston and set of rings for your motor cycle.

14.—You are secretary of your school Photographic Society, and have received the following letter. Write a suitable reply, with an appropriate heading and date, not exceeding 120 words.

" Dear Smith,

I see from the notice board that the Committee propose raising the Photographic Society subscription from 4/- to 5/- per annum. I wish to protest strongly. I have been a member for a few years and I consider that I get less value for my subscription now than I did when it was only 2/6.

I consider that economies could be made and money saved, thus making it unnecessary to pay a higher subscription.

Yours sincerely,
RALPH BROWN."
A.E.B. (*Specimen Paper*).

THE WRITING OF AN ESSAY

Since you were quite young, you have been writing compositions, or essays, which were attempts to express yourself in words. This experience is an advantage, for you will have learned something from your mistakes and will have been encouraged by praise for good efforts ; but it is in one way a disadvantage : what you did in the Lower and Middle School is not up to the standard now required. These notes are intended to help you to reach that standard.

The first essential in writing an essay is to THINK—to spend the first five or ten minutes in thinking about the subject of the essay in order that you may know how to tackle it. Just as a dressmaker requires a pattern of the dress she is to make, a builder must have a plan of the house he is to build, your father has to think out how he is to make a hen-run—so every essay must have a PLAN.

Here is the plan of one of G. K. Chesterton's best essays : " What I found in my pocket."

INTRODUCTION : a well-known saying and reply. " A man can't get on nowadays by hanging about with his hands in his pockets." " I have only once in my life picked a pocket and then I picked my own."

THE OCCASION : A railway carriage—nothing to read—takes things out of his pockets.

CONTENTS, AND COMMENTS : (1) tram-tickets, with advertisements ; (2) pocket-knife ; (3) matches ; (4) chalk ; (5) coin.

CONCLUSION : What he did not find—railway ticket.

You will see that the plan is quite a simple one which has been followed countless times, and it will encourage you to know that the simpler the plan, the better ; but there must be a plan. Your essay must have a beginning, a middle and an ending.

With that warning, let us now consider the essays set recently by the Joint Matriculation Board.

Candidates are recommended to spend not more than 60 minutes on this question.

Write from **two** to **three** pages on **one** of the following subjects :

(a) A fair on Saturday night.

(b) Occasions I detest.

(c) The influence of the sun on our daily lives.

(d) Through which do we obtain more pleasure, our eyes or our ears ?

(e) A discussion between two School Certificate candidates about whether to leave school or go on to the sixth form.

(f) A letter describing your daily life to a boy or girl in another country.

[Note the length required. Two pages at least should be written ; time will not allow you to write much more than three pages.]

First of all, you must choose a subject ; and then forget all about the other subjects. Too often candidates complain of the difficulty of the essay-subjects as though every subject must be attempted. If you find one subject you can write on, be content. Which will you choose ?

If possible choose a subject that is within your experience, because you are likely to write well about what happened to you, or what interests you or in expressing your own feelings.

(a) A fair on Saturday night.

If you have been to a fair recently you should do well on this subject. Don't be afraid to use your imagination ; you may profitably add to reality details from fairs you have read about. This is the privilege of the creator, for art improves on nature.

An obvious plan would be :

INTRODUCTION : Setting out and arrival (don't forget the noises and colour of the fair).

BODY : The Roundabouts and Swings
The Stalls
The fair people
The crowd.—Why are they at the fair ?

CONCLUSION : Going home.

These are the dry bones which you must make live by your descriptive powers.

(b) Occasions I detest.

Note the title—not tasks, such as homework or going errands, but events which happen only occasionally, such as a visit to the dentist, the return from a holiday, being measured for a new suit, going to the barber's.

With three or four such " occasions " you have three or four paragraphs for the main body of the essay.

Such an essay should be written with gusto, for " detest " is a strong word.

(c) The influence of the sun on our daily lives.

INTRODUCTION :   Comment on English weather.

MAIN BODY :   (i) The sun in the country—growing of
                      crops.
                 (ii) In our gardens—making the most of the
                      sun in greenhouses and with cloches.
                (iii) At the seaside. The difference the sun
                      makes to a holiday.
                 (iv) In towns. The first sunny day of
                      spring—influence on our health and
                      spirits.
                  (v) We import the fruits of the sun from
                      other countries.

CONCLUSION :   Sun-worship not surprising.

(d) Through which do we obtain the more pleasure, our
    eyes or our ears ?

An essay in two parts—eyes and ears. In deciding upon the
answer to the question, you should have tabulated a few points
in favour of each.
e.g. " eyes " all a blind man misses—the beauty of the
              world of nature—the sight of friendly faces :
     " ears " bird-song—pleasures of conversation—radio.
If you decide for " eyes " then you may begin with a paragraph about " ears " to show that you realise that through the
ears some pleasure is obtained.
Then develop, with reasons, your argument about " eyes."

(e) A discussion between two School Certificate candidates
    about whether to leave school or go on to the sixth
    form.

Again two points of view, but this time with more balance,
since each side will speak in turn, perhaps to answer the
previous argument, or to develop a new one. If you have a
definite opinion one way or other, you will probably try to
defeat your opponent ; but give him a fair hearing.

(f) A letter describing your daily life to a boy or girl in another country.

If you have a foreign correspondent you have probably written such a letter. Then write to him or her, in France or U.S.A., in as natural a manner as possible.

Remember the letter formalities of address, salutation and ending.

" Your daily life " gives the shape—a time—sequence—a typical day from rising to going to bed. The main difficulty is choice of material which will be interesting to a foreigner because it is different from his life ; e.g. the food you eat, the school you go to, the subjects you take, the games you play.

SUBJECTS FOR ESSAYS

Write two or three pages on **one** of these :

SET 1.

> The Lifeboat Service.
> Machinery, a blessing or a curse ?
> Signalling, past and present.
> Growing up.
> Shadows.
> School Magazines.

SET 2.

> Planning a garden.
> Market Day.
> The fascination of a department store.
> Your favourite weekly or monthly periodical.
> Famous bridges.
> A great reformer.

SET 3.

> Labour-saving devices in modern life.
> The romance of a lump of coal.
> Captive beasts and birds.

Desert islands.

A room of one's own.

The housing problem.

SET 4.

Desirable features of a newly-planned town.

Camouflage.

My private ambitions.

Wonders of bird life.

Crowds.

A speech to be made at a meeting of a debating society for or against the motion : "That both boys and girls should be taught cooking and housewifery."

SET 5.

Time-measuring devices past and present.

Fishing.

Colour in our cities.

Bells.

Patent medicines.

"What's lost upon the roundabouts we pulls up on the swings."

SET 6.

My oldest or youngest relative.

By the river.

Preparing for a camp.

A speech for **or** against the motion that motorists are mainly responsible for road accidents.

The best way to travel.

The use and misuse of pockets.

SET 7.

The advantages which man derives from trees.

Wheels.

My School Sports Day.

What I admire in the character of . . . . (Insert the name of any famous man or woman.)

The sounds of the town and of the country.

(All the above subjects are taken from papers set by the Joint Matriculation Board.)

SET 8.

   (a) The pollution of rivers.

   (b) Street lighting, past and present.

   (c) The importance to Man of the Internal Combustion Engine.

   (d) Reforms and improvements necessary on British Railways.

   (e) The attractions which Great Britain has to offer visitors from overseas.

SET 9.

   (a) Hydro-electric power in the British Isles.

   (b) *Either*,   A townsman in the country.
          or,   A countryman in town.

   (c) The problems of the roads in Great Britain.

   (d) Should men and women receive the same pay for the same work ?

   (e) Maps.

SET 10.

   (a) Develop an argument between two fathers whether it is wise to have a television in a home where there are children of school age.

   (b) Account for the high reputation of the British motor cycle.

   (c) Olympic Games and international sport.

   (d) The holiday that went wrong.

   (e) A gipsy encampment.

   (f) Write an account of what you consider to be the most important development in any one science during this century.

SET 11.

   (a) Indicate the character and contents of any technical periodical in which you are interested.

   (b) ' British films have nothing to learn from Hollywood.'

   (c) What have the western democracies done to assist in

the development of the backward areas of the world, and what more could they do ?

(d) Which kind of summer holiday do you prefer, and why ?

(e) The effects of climate on national life and customs.

(f) ' The Scientist should study English.'

SET 12.

(a) The region you would choose for a national park.

(b) " Mass production and mass distribution must go hand in hand." What are your opinions on this statement ?

(c) The building of satellite towns.

(d) Describe a notable example of civil engineering with which you are acquainted.

(e) Discuss the proposal that the metric system should be introduced into this country.

(f) Our Electrical Grid System.

SET 13.

(a) " The application of science to entertainment has made us lazy." Do you agree or disagree ?

(b) Given the opportunity, in what branch of engineering would you wish to experiment, and why ? Suggest one or more lines of research.

(c) How, in your opinion, may the schoolboy's interest in railway engines be turned to good account ?

(d) " Much of our most valuable natural asset is wasted up the chimney."

Discuss this statement and suggest how the wastage of coal could be minimized.

(e) Your idea of an educated man or woman.

SET 14.

(a) One must move with the times.

(b) Describe some of the difficulties which now prevent interplanetary travel.

(c) How is a trade union organized, what are its functions, and how does it achieve its objects ?

D

(d) Red-letter days of my life.

(e) Television followed sound broadcasting only after a number of years. By comparing the scientific principles involved in each, try to account for this delay.

J.M.B.

SET 15.

(a) Good and bad methods of advertising.

(b) " In this age of machinery there is no place for the craftsman." To what extent is this true ?

(c) Write a letter to the editor of a paper complaining of the lack of facilities in your district for ' keeping fit,' and making suggestions to remedy this lack.

(d) Smugglers—ancient and modern.

(e) A character study of someone who has influenced you greatly.

(f) A great feat of engineering.

(g) Imagine yourself to be an inventor or explorer living in the past, present or future, who after long effort has achieved his aim. Give extracts from the diary in which you recorded your progress.

(h) An architect is to plan a house for you. Tell him what special features you would like him to include.

(i) Write for your school magazine a report on a school activity in which you have taken part.

A.E.B. (*Specimen Paper*).

The following questions have been set in the General Paper of the Joint Matriculation Board.

SET 16.

(a) Give an account of the duties and assess the importance to the community of **Two** of the following : (*a*) a bank manager, (*b*) an accountant, (*c*) a solicitor, (*d*) a headmaster or headmistress.

(b) Discuss the changes which have taken place in the status of women in the last fifty years.

(c) What are the present functions and composition of the

House of Lords ? What changes do you think would be advantageous ?

(d) Discuss the advantages and disadvantages of a two-party parliamentary system.

(e) " If citizens are to be made more equal, they are likely to become less free : if they are left free, they will soon cease to be equal." Comment on this statement.

SET 17.

(a) Write a brief introductory chapter to a guide-book of the county you know best.

(b) Describe some of the effects which the applications of science are having on the appearance of the country-side and the lives of its inhabitants.

(c) To what extent is intellectual curiosity a sufficient motive for scientific enquiry ?

(d) Do you think the prevailing standards of design in things used in everyday life are satisfactory ? Try to account for any defects you mention, and to suggest how quality could be improved.

(e) Explain the meaning of **Five** of the following phrases and show that you recognise the allusion in each phrase you select : (a) a Gilbertian situation, (b) a Machiavellian scheme, (c) a Job's comforter, (d) a gargantuan feast, (e) puckish humour, (f) a quixotic action, (g) a Utopian scheme, (h) a Homeric struggle, (i) Olympian calm.

SET 18.

(a) The average age of the population of this country is rising. Discuss the economic and social effects of this trend.

(b) Discuss, in relation to one another the meanings of the words ' law ' and ' rule ' in the following phrases : a scientific law, a law of the realm, a grammatical rule, a rule of a game.

(c) Point out some of the problems involved in the preserva-tion, packing and transport of foods.

(d) Give a short account of recent advances in **Two** of the following : increasing the speed of aircraft, the remote control of aircraft, weather forecasting, the development of radio astronomy, pest control, the production of new textiles, the estimation of the age of objects excavated by archaeologists.

(e) What contributions can scientists make towards the solution of the problem of securing an adequate food supply for a rapidly increasing world population ?

SET 19.

(a) Discuss the problems of making a film from *either* a novel *or* a play.

Illustrate your answer by reference to not more than two films.

(b) Describe the changes which took place in the style of *either* English clothes *or* English furniture from any century you select to the succeeding century, and suggest why these changes occurred. (You may use sketches.)

(c) " The conventions of opera make it too absurd to be be enjoyable." What conventions are employed in opera ? Say whether you agree or disagree with the statement quoted, and why.

(d) Choose **Two** painters **or** schools of painting, and show what light is thrown by the work of each on the interests and values of the community in which it was produced.

SET 20.

(a) " One man's meat is another man's poison."

" Beauty is not merely in the eye of the beholder."

State these two opinions about the nature of beauty in your own words. Give your own opinion and your reasons for holding it.

(b) Give a reasoned case for **or** against allowing television to be used for advertising.

(c) Discuss the causes of juvenile delinquency and make

one suggestion which might be helpful in dealing with it.

(d) Explain how insurance works. What risks are commonly insured against in this country ?

(e) What problems does road traffic in this country give rise to ? Which suggestions for dealing with them do you think most worth trying ?

SET 21.

(a) " Strike and lock-outs are obsolete methods of settling industrial disputes." Discuss.

(b) What is a comprehensive school ? Give reasons for or against making most secondary schools comprehensive.

(c) Can there be any justification for scientific research which has no practical end in view ?

(d) Give an account of the work of One of the following, explaining its importance : Mendel, John Dalton, Sir Frank Whittle, Lord Rutherford and Pasteur.

(e) What uses are being made of radio-active substances produced at atomic energy stations ?

(f) Write notes on Two of the following :
(a) blood transfusion, (b) detergents, (c) " Smog "
(d) warm and cold fronts, (e) short and long sight,
(f) science in the detection of crime.

Part Seven: PRÉCIS WRITING

The manufacturers of a glue paste gave instructions on the tin :

" The best results from the application of this paste will be obtained by the minimum amount taken on the brush and spread evenly over the surface."

Then somebody noticed that the same information could be given in two words :

" Apply thinly."

and the change was made.

This is a simple example of the Précis.

The Précis is a very useful form of composition, in which we are required to give a summary of a passage in about a third or quarter of its original length. The ability to do this has great practical value, for whenever we tell our friends about a book we have read or a film we have seen we are attempting a précis. Similarly, when we hear a speech, sermon or lesson, our mind makes a summary and our memory stores it for future reference.

Therefore it is important that we should train our minds to choose the essentials of what we read.

Précis writing is not easy ; but practice and the observance of certain points will help.

(1) Read through the passage at least twice.

(2) Decide which are the most important points and make short notes of these, to serve as a skeleton round which to build the précis.

(3) Make the first draft, observing 4, 5, 6, 7.

(4) Keep the same order of ideas as in the original ; add no comment or idea that is not in the original.

(5) Omit, or drastically reduce, illustrations and figures of speech.

(6) Avoid, as much as possible, the copying of phrases and sentences from the original.

(7) The précis may be written in direct or indirect speech, whichever is the more convenient, but speeches and letters should be in indirect speech. In the examination paper specific instructions are sometimes given.

(8) When the first draft is made, examine it for length. It is much easier to shorten a draft than to lengthen one too short.

(9) See that it reads smoothly, with no grammatical errors. The importance of style in a précis is often overlooked. It is just as important to write well in a précis as in an essay.

(10) Write the final draft.

SPECIMEN

Make a précis of the following passage in about one-third of its length.

For there is a perennial nobleness, and even sacredness, in Work. Were he never so benighted, forgetful of his high calling there is always hope in a man that actually and earnestly works : in Idleness alone is there perpetual despair. Work, never so Mammonish, mean, *is* in communication with Nature ; the real desire to get work done will itself lead one more and more to truth, to Nature's appointments and regulations, which are truth.

The latest Gospel in this World is know thy work and do it. " Know thyself " : long enough has that poor " self " of thine tormented thee : thou wilt never get to " know " it, I believe ! Think it not thy business, this of knowing thyself ; thou art an unknowable individual : know what thou canst work at ; and work at it, like a Hercules ! That will be thy better plan.

It has been written, " an endless significance lies in Work " ; a man perfects himself by working. Foul jungles are cleared away, fair seedfields rise instead, and stately cities ; and withal the man himself first ceases to be a jungle and foul unwholesome desert thereby. Consider how, even in the meanest sorts of Labour, the whole soul of man is composed into a kind of real harmony, the instant he sets himself to work ! Doubt, Desire, Sorrow, Remorse, Indignation, Despair itself, all these like helldogs lie beleaguering the soul of the poor day-worker, as of every man : but he bends himself with free valour against his task, and all these are stilled, all these shrink murmuring far off into their caves. The man is now a man. The blessed glow of Labour in him, is it not as purifying fire, wherein all poison is burnt up, and of sour smoke itself there is made bright blessed flame !

Destiny, on the whole, has no other way of cultivating us. A formless Chaos, once set it *revolving*, grows round and ever rounder ; ranges itself, by mere force of gravity, into strata, spherical courses ; it is no longer a Chaos, but a round compacted World. What would become of the Earth, did she cease to revolve ? In the poor old Earth, as long as she revolves, all inequalities, irregularities, disperse themselves ; all irregularities are incessantly becoming regular. Hast thou looked on the Potter's wheel—one of the venerablest objects ; old as the Prophet Ezekiel and far older ? Rude lumps of clay, how they spin themselves up, by mere quick whirling, into beautiful circular dishes. And fancy the most assiduous Potter, but without his wheel ; reduced to make dishes, or rather amorphous botches, by mere kneading and baking ! Even such a Potter were Destiny, with a human soul that would rest and lie at ease, that would not work and spin ! Of an idle unrevolving man the kindest Destiny, like the most assiduous Potter without wheel, can bake and knead nothing other than a botch ; let her spend on him what expensive colouring, what gilding and enamelling she will, he is but a botch. Not a dish ; no, a bulging, kneaded, crooked, shambling, squint-cornered, amorphous botch—a mere enamelled vessel of dishonour ! Let the idle think of this. (526 words)

Past and Present : THOMAS CARLYLE

Outline

1.—Work is natural to man.

2.—Find the type of work you are capable of.

3.—Work has good influences upon man.

4.—Using a comparison with the earth's evolution from chaos and an image of the potter's wheel, we become what we are through the work we do.

First Draft

Carlyle says there is a perennial nobleness about Work. Even if we work merely for our wages or profits we are doing something natural which will lead us to discover the laws of Nature which are the basis of truth.

Man can never know himself, but he can find the work he can do and he can devote himself to that.

Man fulfils himself through work. Man has cultivated the waste places and has developed the civilisation he enjoys. However humble a man's work may be, it creates a harmony in the soul of man which drives away the many cares and sorrows which trouble him.

It is only through work that Destiny can develop our character. This world has been made from chaos and, following natural laws it revolves and changes. The work of nature cannot stop. Just as the potter uses his ever-whirling wheel to create from lumps of clay beautiful pottery, so through our work we are made men. If we are idle we are worth little.

(170 words)

This is right for length, but it needs polishing. Some phrases are too much like the original. The mixture of " we " and " he " is to be avoided.

Final Draft

Carlyle says that work is a great and dignified activity. Even if man works merely for wages or profits, he is doing something natural which will lead him to discover the laws of Nature which are the basis of truth.

D*

Man can never really understand himself, but he can find the work he can do and devote himself to that.

Man proves himself through work. He has cultivated the waste places and has developed the civilisation he enjoys. However humble the work may be, it creates in the soul of man a harmony which makes him forget the many cares and sorrows which trouble him.

It is only through work that Destiny can develop character. This world was made from chaos and, following natural laws, it revolves and changes. The work of nature cannot stop. Just as the ever-whirling wheel is necessary to the potter who creates from lumps of clay beautiful pottery, so it is through work that the spirit of man finds fulfilment. If men are idle they are worth little.   (173 words)

PASSAGES FOR PRÉCIS

[More précis work will be found in the exercises on Understanding.]

Where no instructions are given, summarise in about one-third of the length of the original. Supply a title.

I

Rewrite this description in about 60 words.

The ring-formed reef of the lagoon-island is surmounted in the greater part of its length by linear islets. On the northern or leeward side, there is an opening through which vessels can pass to the anchorage within. On entering, the scene was very curious and rather pretty ; its beauty, however, entirely depended on the brilliancy of the surrounding colours. The shallow, clear, and still water of the lagoon, resting in its greater part on white sand, is, when illumined by a vertical sun, of the most vivid green. This brilliant expanse, several miles in width, is on all sides divided, either by a line of snow-white breakers from the dark heaving waters of the ocean, or from the blue vault of heaven by the strips of land, crowned by the level tops of the cocoa-nut trees. As a white cloud here and there affords a pleasing contrast with the azure sky, so, in the lagoon, bands of living coral darken the emerald-green water.

The Voyage of the Beagle : CHARLES DARWIN

2

Give the sense of this passage in about of 60 of your own words.

" There is a pleasure in painting which none but painters know." In writing you have to contend with the world ; in painting, you have only to carry on a friendly strife with Nature. You sit down to your task, and are happy. From the moment you take up the pencil, and look Nature in the face, you are at peace with your own heart. No angry passions rise to disturb the silent progress of the work, to shake the hand, or dim the brow : no irritable humours are set afloat ; you have no absurd opinions to combat, no point to strain, no adversary to crush, no fool to annoy—you are actuated by fear or favour to no man. There is " no juggling here," no sophistry, no intrigue, no tampering with the evidence, no attempt to make black white, or white black : but you resign yourself into the hands of a greater power, that of Nature, with the simplicity of a child, and the devotion of an enthusiast— " study with joy her manner, and with rapture her style."

WILLIAM HAZLITT

3

For the soldier's trade, verily and essentially, is not slaying, but being slain. This, without well knowing its own meaning, the world honours it for. A bravo's trade is slaying ; but the world has never respected bravos more than merchants : the reason it honours the soldier is because he holds his life at the service of the State. Reckless he may be—fond of pleasure or of adventure—all kinds of bye-motives and mean impulses may have determined the choice of his profession, and may affect (to all appearance exclusively) his daily conduct in it ; but our estimate of him is based on this ultimate fact—of which we are well assured—that, put him in a fortress breach, with all the pleasures of the world behind him, and only death and

his duty in front of him, he will keep his face to the front ;
and he knows that this choice may be put to him at any
moment, and has beforehand taken his part—virtually takes
such part continually—does, in reality, die daily. (176 words)
Unto This Last : RUSKIN

4

It was not so much his uncommon bulk that so much
distinguished him from other sperm-whales, but a peculiar
snow-white wrinkled forehead, and a high, pyramidical white
hump. These were his prominent features ; the tokens whereby he revealed his identity, at a long distance, to those who
knew him.

The rest of his body was so streaked, and spotted, and
marbled with the same shrouded hue, that, in the end, he had
gained his distinctive appellation of the White Whale ; a
name, indeed, literally justified by his vivid aspect, when seen
gliding at high noon through a dark blue sea, leaving a milky
wake of creamy foam, all spangled with golden gleamings.
Nor was it his unwonted magnitude, nor his remarkable hue,
nor yet his deformed lower jaw, that so much invested the
whale with natural terror, as that unexampled, intelligent
malignity which, according to specific accounts, he had over
and over again evinced in his assaults. More than all, his
treacherous retreats struck more of dismay than perhaps aught
else. For, when swimming before his exulting pursuers, with
every apparent symptom of alarm, he had several times been
known to turn round suddenly, and bearing down upon them,
either stave their boats to splinters, or drive them back in
consternation to their ship.   (213 words)
Moby Dick : HERMAN MELVILLE

5

Give the sense of this passage in between sixty and seventy
words :

And sooth to say, when I surveyed my mass of evidence,
whether derived from vivisections, and my various reflections
on them, or from the ventricles of the heart and the vessels

that enter into and issue from them, the symmetry and size of these conduits—for Nature doing nothing in vain, would never have given them so large a relative size without a purpose—or from the arrangement and intimate structure of the valves in particular, and of the other parts of the valves in general, with many things besides, I frequently and seriously bethought me, and long resolved in my mind what might be the quantity of blood which was transmitted, in how short a time its passage might be effected, and the like ; and not finding it possible that this could be supplied by the juices of the ingested aliment without the veins on the one hand becoming drained, and the arteries on the other getting ruptured through the excessive charge of blood, unless the blood should somehow find its way from the arteries into the veins, and so return to the right side of the heart ; I began to think whether there might not be *a motion, as it were, in a circle.*

The Circulation of the Blood : W. HARVEY

6

Write a précis, in about one third of its length, of the following passage.

What are the great advantages of plastics over other materials ? First of all is the comparative ease with which they are shaped. Articles varying in size from the head of a drawing-pin to a complete motor-car body can be pressed out one after another. For some of the stronger articles heating may be necessary for as long as an hour, but for most it is a matter of a few minutes or even seconds. Then there is the fact that they finish with a high polish. Wood usually needs elaborate polishing and constant repolishing. The plastic article is 'born polished' and will retain its gloss almost indefinitely, requiring, at the most, washing to remove grease and dirt.

Although plastics require no actual polishing, most of them will take a dye very easily in the manufacturing process and can therefore be used for decorative purposes. The dye is generally incorporated at the grinding stage, when the dried resin is reduced to powder and mixed with a filler. Almost any desired colour can be produced, and it will be absolutely fast. Moreover, methods of mixing dyes enable attractive designs of colours which ' run ' into each other to be produced. These dyes are so firmly fixed in the substances that they do not affect the taste of food served on plastic dishes. The plastic itself resists the attacks of such acids as are found in food and of alkalis of moderate strength.

Then we have the individual properties of the different plastics. Some, like bakelite, are remarkable for their insulating properties and form a good substitute for glass or rubber in electrical apparatus. Perhaps the word ' substitute ' is not correct, for it generally implies something inferior, whereas plastics have electrical properties equal to the older insulators, and other properties, such as strength and permanence, vastly superior. Some plastics are valued for their great tensile strength, which may be as much as 12,000 lb. per square inch ; others for their heat-resisting qualities, or for their transparency.

(approx. 330 words.)
Science in Industry : A. M. Low

7

Make a précis of this passage in about one third of its length.

We often say ' as light as air ' as if air were nothing at all ; whereas, at the earth's surface the air is quite heavy. Because it is transparent we are apt to forget its presence, yet we soon feel its motion, and when there is a high wind it may blow us over. If we travel on something that moves quickly we find that the air offers resistance. A motor-car or aeroplane must cut its way through the air, and so is streamlined in order that the air may flow freely round it. It is the resistance of the air that makes the parachute descend slowly. It sails gently downwards because the weight it supports is spread out over its huge canopy, which cannot fall more rapidly because the invisible air is sufficiently dense to resist the motion of so large a surface.

The air we breathe is merely the lower and denser part of the atmosphere which encircles the earth. The air around us we take for granted, without thinking specially about it, yet it is essential to our existence. If we could not breathe we should soon die. But the atmosphere serves other purposes besides ; it helps to maintain a fairly even temperature, so that over most of the world it is neither so hot that life is scorched, nor so cold that everything freezes. It acts as a screen to shield us from harmful rays that would otherwise beat down on the earth and make life impossible. It also protects us from the myriads of small fragments called meteors which continually rain down upon the earth from outer space.

We always think of the surface of the earth as being the natural environment for mankind ; but there are many dead worlds, like the moon, where, for want of an atmosphere, no human being could live. It is the atmosphere therefore that gives us life and protection ; that warms and shields us by night from the fierce cold of outer space ; that gives us all the changes of weather, and softens the blinding glare of the sun by day, diffusing and spreading the varied light and colour of the open air.   (360 words.)

The Atmosphere : P. Hood

8

In the calm days of summer the Ojibwa fisherman pushes out his birch canoe upon the great inland ocean of the north ; and, as he gazes down into the pellucid depths, he seems like one balanced between earth and sky. The watchful fish-hawk circles above his head ; and below, farther than his line will reach, he sees the trout glide shadowy and silent over the glimmering pebbles. The little islands on the verge of the horizon seem now starting into spires, now melting into a thousand fantastic forms, with the strange mirage of the waters ; and he fancies that the evil spirits of the lake lie basking their serpent forms on those unhallowed shores. Again, he explores the watery labyrinths where the stream sweeps among pine-tufted islands, or runs, black and deep, beneath the shadows of moss-bearded firs ; or he lifts his canoe upon the sandy beach, and, while his camp-fire crackles on the grass-flat, reclines beneath the trees, and smokes and laughs away the sultry hours, in a lazy luxury of enjoyment.

But when winter descends upon the north, sealing up the fountains, fettering the streams, and turning the green-robed forests to shivering nakedness, then, bearing their frail dwellings upon their backs, the Ojibwa family wander forth into the wilderness, cheered only on their dreary track by the whistling of the north wind, and the hungry howl of wolves. By the banks of some frozen stream, women and children, men and dogs, lie crouched together around the fire. They spread their benumbed fingers over the embers, while the wind shrieks through the fir-trees like the gale through the rigging of a frigate, and the narrow concave of the wigwam sparkles with the frost-work of their congealed breath. In vain they beat the magic drum, and call upon their guardian manitous ; the wary moose keeps aloof, the bear lies close in his hollow tree, and famine stares them in the face. And now the hunter can fight no more against the nipping cold and blinding sleet. Stiff and stark, with haggard cheek and shrivelled lip, he lies among the snow drifts ; till with tooth and claw, the famished wildcat strives in vain to pierce the frigid marble of his limbs. Such harsh schooling is thrown away on the incorrigible mind of the northern Algonquin. He lives in misery, as his fathers lived before him. Still, in the brief hour of plenty he forgets the season of want ; and still the sleet and the snow descend upon his houseless head.   (434 words.)

Conspiracy of Pontiac : PARKMAN

9

If ever I saw anything like actual migration, it was last Michaelmas Day. I was travelling, and out early in the morning ; at first there was a vast fog, but, by the time that I was got seven or eight miles from home towards the coast, the sun broke out into a delicate warm day. We were then on a large heath or common, and I could discern, as the mist began to break away, great numbers of swallows (*hirundines rusticæ*) clustering on the stunted shrubs and bushes, as if they had roosted there all night. As soon as the air became clear and pleasant they were all on the wing at once ; and, by a placid and easy flight, proceeded on southward towards the sea ; after this I did not see any more flocks, only now and then a straggler.

I cannot agree with those persons that assert that the swallow kind disappear some and some gradually as they come, for the bulk of them seem to withdraw at once ; only some stragglers stay behind a long while, and do never, there is the greatest reason to believe, leave this island. Swallows seem to lay themselves up, and to come forth in a warm day, as bats do continually of a warm evening after they have disappeared for weeks. For a very respectable gentleman assured me that, as he was walking with some friends under Merton Hall on a remarkably hot noon either in the last week in December or the first week in January, he espied three or four swallows huddled together on the moulding of one of the windows of that college. I have frequently remarked that swallows are seen later at Oxford than elsewhere ; is it owing to the vast massy buildings of that place, to the many waters round it, or to what else ?

When I used to rise in the morning last autumn, and see the swallows and martins clustering on the chimneys and thatch of the neighbouring cottages, I could not help being touched with a secret delight, mixed with some degree of mortification ; with delight, to observe with how much ardour and punctuality those poor little birds obeyed the strong impulse towards migration, or hiding, imprinted on their minds by their great Creator ; and with some degree of mortification, when I reflected that, after all our pains and inquiries, we are yet not quite certain to what regions they do migrate ; and are still farther embarrassed to find that some do not actually migrate at all.   (424 words.)

Natural History of Selborne : GILBERT WHITE

10

Mankind, in the first ages of society, before the establishment of law, order, and security, have little curiosity to find out those hidden chains of events which bind together the seemingly disjointed appearances of nature. A savage, whose subsistence is precarious, whose life is every day exposed to the rudest dangers, has no inclination to amuse himself with searching out what, when discovered, seems to serve no other purpose than to render the theatre of nature a more connected spectacle to his imagination. Many of these smaller incoherences, which in the course of things perplex philosophers, entirely escape his attention. Those more magnificent irregularities, whose grandeur he cannot overlook, call forth his amazement. Comets, eclipses, thunder, lightning and other meteors by their greatness naturally overawe him, and he views them with a reverence that approaches to fear. His inexperience and uncertainty with regard to everything about them, how they came, how they are to go, what went before, what is to come after them, exasperate his sentiment into terror and consternation. But our passions, as Father Malebranche observes, all justify themselves ; that is, suggest to us opinions which justify them. As those appearances terrify him, therefore he is disposed to believe everything about them which can render them still more the objects of his terror. That they proceed from some intelligent though invisible causes, of whose vengeance and displeasure they are either the signs or the effects, is the notion of all others most capable of enhancing this passion, and is that therefore which he is most apt to entertain. To this, too, that cowardice and pusillanimity, so natural to man in his uncivilised state, still more disposes him : unprotected by the laws of society, exposed, defenceless, he feels his weakness upon all occasions ; his strength and security upon none. (203 words)

Essay on the History of Astronomy : Adam Smith

II

The death of Nelson was felt in England as something more than a public calamity : men started at the intelligence and turned pale, as if they had heard of the loss of a dear friend. An object of our admiration and affection, of our pride and of our hopes, was suddenly taken from us ; and it seemed as if we had never, till then, known how deeply we loved and reverenced him. What the country had lost in its great naval hero—the greatest of our own and of all former times—was scarcely taken into the account of grief. So perfectly indeed had he performed his part that the maritime war, after the battle of Trafalgar, was considered at an end : the fleets of the enemy were not merely defeated, but destroyed ; new navies must be built, and a new race of seamen reared for them, before the possibility of their invading our shores could again be contemplated. It was not therefore from any selfish reflection upon the magnitude of our loss that we mourned for him ; the general sorrow was of a higher character. The people of England grieved that funeral ceremonies and public monuments and posthumous awards were all they could bestow upon whom the king, the legislature, and the nation would have alike delighted to honour ; whom every tongue would have blessed ; whose presence in every village through which he might have passed would have wakened the church-bells, have given schoolboys a holiday, have drawn children from their sports to gaze upon him, and " old men from the chimney corner " to look upon Nelson ere they died. The victory of Trafalgar was celebrated indeed with the usual forms of rejoicing, but they were without joy. . . .

Yet he cannot be said to have fallen prematurely whose work was done ; nor ought he to be lamented who died so full of honours and at the height of human fame. The most triumphant death is that of the martyr ; the most awful, that of the martyred patriot ; the most splendid, that of the hero in the hour of victory : and if the chariot and the horses of fire had been vouchsafed for Nelson's translation, he could scarcely have departed in a brighter blaze of glory. He has left us, not indeed his mantle of inspiration, but a name and an example which are at this hour inspiring thousands of the youth of England—a name which is our pride, and an example which will continue to be our shield and our strength. Thus it is that the spirits of the great and the wise continue to live and to act after them. (357 words)

The Life of Nelson : Southey

12

Write a précis in about 150 words of the following passage.

Only a few years ago packaging would hardly have been deemed a worthy subject to write about. Today it is probably true to say that no other ancillary function is so important to the production, marketing and distribution sides of our national life. What factors have operated to bring about this great change? First, and perhaps most important, was the 1939-1945 World War. In the early days of that conflict vital and costly material arrived at the various theatres of operations in an unusable condition. Millions of pounds were wasted in this way. Only recently, for instance, it was announced that over 90 per cent of the cathode ray tubes sent overseas arrived smashed. Field rations, too, arrived uneatable and this had an incalculable effect on the morale of the troops. In war-time, money and scientific resources are immediately available on a scale that could never be envisaged in peace-time and to this fact alone can be ascribed much of the progress that has been made in the packaging of goods for safe transit, and storage, all over the world.

But there are other aspects beyond preservation packing and packing for export, and the second most important factor is the change, most noticeable in the United States, from counter-service to self-service for all kinds of merchandise. Self-service stores are now coming into favour in this country also, and now the package must not merely contain and store the goods. In the absence of the shop assistants' recommendation, it must sell them too. In fact, it has often been said that, under these conditions, one's competitor is a package and not the article it contains. Thirdly, there has been of late a drive for cleanliness and food hygiene. This has led to an enormous increase in the packaging of all kinds of foods. Fourthly, more modern ideas on the handling and storing of goods, and the increase in the use and availability of road transport, have brought new thoughts on unit packages. These must now fit the handling capacity of the pallets used for fork lift trucks, or be suitable for handling mechanically by conveyor or other methods. In addition, the improved handling usually associated with road transport has led to a widespread increase in the use of fibreboard cartons which are infinitely cheaper and more easily stored than wooden cases. Finally, among the main factors which have led to a far greater awareness of packaging, one must note the work of the Institute of Packaging, born out of the war-time experiences of a group of army officers, the Report and subsequent work of the Anglo-American Productivity Committee's Specialist Team on Packaging which toured the U.S.A. in the winter of 1949-50, and the researches of the Packaging Division of the P.A.T.R.A. Laboratories at Leatherhead.   (approx. 460 words)

E. G. O. RIDGWELL

13

Summarize the following passage in about 190 words :

In England the town was originally, in every case save that of London, a mere bit of land within the lordship, whether of the king or of some great noble or ecclesiastic, whose inhabitants happened, either for purposes of trade or protection, to cluster together more closely than elsewhere. It is this characteristic of our boroughs that separates them at once from the cities of Italy and Provence, which had preserved the municipal institutions of their Roman origins, from the German towns founded by Henry the Fowler with the special purpose of sheltering industry from the feudal oppression around them, or from the French communes which at a later time sprang into existence in sheer revolt against feudal outrage within their walls. In England the tradition of Rome had utterly passed away, while the oppression of feudalism was held fairly in check by the power of the Crown. The English town, therefore, was in its beginning simply a piece of the general country, organized and governed in the same way as the manors around it, that is to say, justice was administered, its annual rent collected, and its customary services extracted by the reeve or steward of the lord to whose estate it belonged. To modern eyes the subjection which these services involved might seem complete. When Leicester, for instance, passed from the hands of the Conqueror into those of its Earls, its townsmen were bound to reap their lord's corn-crops, to grind at his mill, to redeem their strayed cattle from his pound. The great forest around was the Earl's, and it was only out of his grace that the little borough could drive its swine into the woods or pasture its cattle in the glades. The justice and government of the town lay wholly in its master's hands ; he appointed its bailiffs, received the fines and forfeitures of his tenants, and the fees and tolls of their markets and fairs. But when once these dues were paid and these services rendered the English townsman was practically free. His rights were as rigidly defined by custom as those of his lord. Property and person alike were secured against arbitrary seizure. He could demand a fair trial on any charge, and even if justice was administered by his master's reeve it was administered in the presence and with the assent of his fellow-townsmen. The bell which swung out from the town tower gathered the burgesses to a common meeting, where they could exercise rights of free speech and free deliberation on their own affairs. Their merchant-gild, over its ale-feast, regulated trade, distributed the sums due from the town among the different burgesses, looked to the due repairs of gate and wall and acted, in fact, pretty much the same part as a town-council of today.   (469 words)

A Short History of the English People : J. R. GREEN
OXFORD AND CAMBRIDGE

14

What, then, do we ask of an industry ? By what do we judge that industry ? It seems to me that the question can be answered in simple terms. In the first place we expect it to be efficient, for its very purpose is to contribute towards the national income upon which the standard of living depends, and the larger the production per unit of effort the greater the service rendered by the industry to the community. In the circumstances of today it is unnecessary to add to the discussion of the need for efficiency which formed the subject of the first chapter. But efficiency is not to be confounded with uniformity of methods. It has already been shown that the feature of every industry is variety of technique and organisation whether it be efficient or inefficient, quick moving or slow moving, publicly controlled, like the post office and municipal slaughterhouses (one of the strongest and most firmly entrenched vested interests in modern British industry), or privately controlled, like the mining in the past and the cotton industry past and present. It is true of industry not only in this country but throughout the modern world. Progress is determined by the rate of obsolescence adopted in practice; if the true economic rate is in operation the industry is satisfying the criterion of efficiency.

In the second place the industry should provide conditions of employment (broadly interpreted) that compare not unfavourably with those prevailing elsewhere. Some of these, such as unemployment insurance, are taken over by the State ; others, such as provision for safety, are the subject of legal enactment ; some are the subject of collective bargaining and agreement with the trade unions. But these do not relieve the employers of further obligation : in every industrial establishment there are innumerable problems of human relationship and individual conditions of service that are not and cannot be covered in or by general agreements. One, the problem of control, will be discussed later. It is sufficient, at this stage, to point out that every man should treat others as he would hope and expect to be treated if he were in their place.

In the third place the products of the industry should be supplied to the consumers at a reasonable price. This is a question begging phrase : I am as deeply conscious of the fact as any critical reader is likely to be and have myself written and lectured upon the many issues that it raises. Yet my meaning, in broad terms, is clear. There are circumstances in which, by virtue of monopoly and secrecy, an industry may exploit the community or discriminate against parts of it. Effective competition serves as a corrective and makes such exploitation extremely difficult if not quite impossible : monopoly, in certain circumstances, may prove anti-social.

(approx. 380 words)

The Structure of Industry : J. H. JONES

15

Make a précis of the following passage in a version of your own, about 150 words long.

Modern industry in peace or war is founded upon steel, and modern steel-making is founded upon three British inventions. Bessemer in 1856 and Siemens in 1867 established the converter and open-hearth processes for making steel as it is known to-day, but both depended upon the iron ore used being almost free from phosphorus. Most of the world's ores—including most British ones—contain much phosphorus. To make these phosphoric iron ores suitable for steel-making called for a further discovery, the third in the great series. This was made by Sir Gilchrist Thomas, inventor of the basic process, who was born a hundred years ago, on 16th April, 1850.

Like the other two inventions, Thomas's discovery was made outside the industry. " An amateur pressed it upon the iron-makers," as one Middlesbrough iron-master put it. Thomas tried while he was doing his experimental work to get a post as chemist in an ironworks, but he was turned down because he was not a " practical chemist." For the same reason his first application to become a Fellow of the Chemical Society failed. At that time he was a clerk at the Thames Police Court, and his chemical and metallurgical work was done in his spare time. It would be quite wrong, however, to regard the work as merely a hobby. Sensitive, studious and determined, Thomas came of a scholarly and clerical family, with a background of Whig and humanitarian politics. A brilliant all-round scholar at Dulwich, he hoped to study medicine, but the early death of his father forced him to earn his living, first for a short time as a classical master and then as a police court clerk. He experimented at home and soon was convinced of the tremendous importance of dephosphorization. He set out upon his life's great work.

Thomas was not alone in the quest. The general nature of the solution—the use of cheap " basic " materials such as limestone to combine with phosphoric acid when steel was being refined—was already foreseen in the industry. He succeeded in finding the right answer by years of persistent experiment, conducted first at home and later through his cousin Percy Gilchrist—a " practical chemist " at the Welsh Ironworks which had rejected Thomas himself. Success was sure by 1879 and patents were taken out. The first announcement to the Iron and Steel Institute was received in contemptuous and sceptical silence. Within a year, however, the world's steel-makers were eager to follow his lead.

Nearly all the steel made is basic steel. Two world wars have witnessed in this country a greater use not only of basic steel, but also of the Northamptonshire phosphoric ores with which Thomas himself experimented—and which still hardly play the part which they could play in British steelmaking. Thomas overtaxed himself in making his great discovery and died in 1885, only thirty-five years old. He had made money from licences to steelmakers and from the use of basic slag as a fertilizer ; but he had no interest in wealth for himself. The sums earned by " solving the greatest industrial problem of England," as Thomas termed it, were left to relieve distress and to promote reform. They were used under his sister's direction to help a multitude of good causes—among them co-operation, temperance, housing, the provision of open spaces, emigration, and the working conditions of shop assistants and factory girls.   (about 500 words)
" The Times "
(I.C.E. & I.E.E.)

16

The Moon has no detectable atmosphere, and its surface is severely pockmarked, looking as if it had been bombarded by a host of large celestial missiles. And this is very likely just what has happened. At one time it was thought that the lunar craters were extinct volcanoes, but for the following reasons this now seems unlikely. Some of the craters are over a hundred miles across and do not show the same uniformity of structure. Besides, it is certain that volcanic activity on the Moon is quite negligible at the present time.

Perhaps the strongest argument in favour of the bombardment theory is that the amount of material in the walls surrounding a crater can actually be estimated, and it turns out to be just the amount required to fill in the hole in the floor of the crater. But in spite of this patent clue the bombardment theory has not gained general currency because it was thought that a crushing argument could be brought against it. There are large areas of the Moon where no craters can be found. How have all the missiles contrived to miss these areas, whereas in other places the craters are almost overlapping each other ? Only the other day the way round this apparent difficulty was pointed out to me by my colleague, Gold. The fierce heating of the lunar surface rocks by day and the cooling by night must lead to an alternate contraction and expansion which causes small bits of rock to flake away from the surface. These particles of dust tend to work their way to the lower parts of the Moon where they have accumulated as gigantic drifts that cover the underlying craters. I think that this brand new idea is almost certainly correct, because it not only overcomes the old objection, but it also explains those cases where the walls, or only a portion of the walls, of a crater stick straight out of an apparently flat plain. These are simply the cases where the drift of dust is not sufficiently deep to cover the craters entirely.

(350 words)

The Nature of the Universe : F. HOYLE

17

Summarise the following passage in about one-third of its length :

In one respect it must be admitted that the progress of civilisation has diminished the physical comforts of the poorest class. It has already been mentioned that, before the Revolution, many thousands of square miles, now enclosed and cultivated, were marsh, forest, and heath. Of this wild land much was, by law, common, and much of what was not common by law was worth so little that the proprietors suffered it to be common in fact. In such a tract squatters and trespassers were tolerated to an extent now unknown. The peasant who dwelt there could, at little or no charge, procure occasionally some palatable addition to his fare, and provide himself with fuel for the winter. He kept a flock of geese on what is now an orchard rich with apple blossoms. He snared wild fowl on the fen which has long since been drained and divided into corn fields and turnip fields. He cut turf among the furze bushes on the moor which is now a meadow bright with clover and renowned for butter and cheese. The progress of agriculture and the increase of population necessarily deprived him of these privileges. But against this disadvantage a long list of advantages is to be set off. Of the blessings which civilisation and philosophy bring with them a large proportion is common to all ranks, and would, if withdrawn, be missed as painfully by the labourer as by the peer. The market place which the rustic can now reach with his cart in an hour, was, a hundred and sixty years ago, a day's journey from him. The street which now affords to the artisan, during the whole night, a secure, a convenient, and a brilliantly lighted walk was, a hundred and sixty years ago, so dark after sunset that he would not have been able to see his hand, so ill paved that he would have run constant risk of breaking his neck, and so ill watched that he would have been in imminent danger of being knocked down and plundered of his small earnings. Every bricklayer who falls from a scaffold, every sweeper of a crossing who is run over by a carriage, may now have his wounds dressed and his limbs set with a skill such as, a hundred and sixty years ago, all the wealth of a great lord like Ormond, or of a merchant prince like Clayton, could not have purchased. Some frightful diseases have been extirpated by science ; and some have been banished by police. The term of human life has been lengthened over the whole kingdom, and especially in the towns.

(437 words)

The State of England in 1685 : MACAULAY
OXFORD AND CAMBRIDGE

18

Make a précis of the following passage in about one-third of its length.

The B.B.C. was established by Royal Charter to conduct broadcasting as a public service. The Charter says nothing specific about the meaning of this expression, though it refers to the value of the programmes transmitted by the Corporation as a means of informing, educating, and entertaining the people of the United Kingdom. The aims and responsibilities of public-service broadcasting were gradually crystallised by the founders and pioneers of broadcasting in the B.B.C., and have been accepted through the years not only by the public, but the various Parliamentary Commissions that have examined the B.B.C.'s operations, and by opinion abroad, where the B.B.C.'s reputation stands very high among broadcasting organisations and among its world-wide audience. I should define these aims and responsibilities as follows.

First, the B.B.C. should develop to the maximum the potentialities of broadcasting as a means of communication. There should be a constant effort to think out new ways in which information, interest, and enjoyment can be conveyed. The value of any programme resides in its content, whether it be grave or gay, serious or trivial. But however good the content, the programme fails unless it is put into a form in which people can absorb it. The challenge to the broadcaster is perpetually there—how can every programme be made to arouse the maximum interest and enjoyment ?

Second, the B.B.C. must try to satisfy the needs and tastes of the full range of listeners and viewers. The public is not a uniform mass of people, but a great company of individuals with an almost infinite variety of interests, inclinations, enthusiasms, dislikes and prejudices. We have to try to achieve a similar variety in the programmes we present. To express the situation in a negative way : something would be wrong if any one individual, however representative, found that he liked all the programmes.

Third, the B.B.C. in its several programme services should include all types of material that it is possible to convey by broadcasting, provided that in each field the aim should be to search constantly for the best available. Much has already been done in this way, partly because of the great progress that has been made in communications and in the opening up of sources from which programmes can be drawn, and partly because of the development of programme forms which has made it possible to present a much wider range of subjects. As television gets into its stride, still more can be done.

Fourth, the B.B.C. should try so to enlighten listeners and viewers that they will tend to prefer what is best. This doesn't mean that we should thrust down people's throats what we believe to be good for them at the expense of what they want. It means that every opportunity should be taken to lay before the audience, in each field of output, examples of the highest standard so that in the process of time they will come to reject that which falls below it. Many new vistas can be opened by broadcasting, and people may be enabled to explore some of which they were previously unaware. But the aim here is not so much to change tastes and interests as to raise them to the highest level of which they are capable.

Finally, the B.B.C. should embrace the world in its operations while remaining responsive to national needs as these become evident.   (approx. 560 words)
                                              SIR IAN JACOB

19

Write a précis of this passage in about a third of its length.

The world does not owe Britain a living. We shall always—and in future more so—have to earn our British standard of life in competition. No one need love us. Ingratitude is a more general human characteristic than gratitude—as Americans can certainly testify from their experience in the past five years, and as the British can testify from theirs in the past hundred.

Besides, everything we decide to do in our domestic affairs must inevitably have more of an effect upon our standard of life than would be the case in any other nation. We depend more on world trading than any other nation. Whatever we do inside our own boundaries will automatically affect the output of this or that group of British subjects engaged in their differing walks of life, all of which walks lead to world trade. A fall in the productivity of commercial clerks or bank managers in Britain would be as dangerous to our standard of life as a fall in the efficiency of coal-miners or dockers. A falling-off in the effective skill of factory managers, accountants, financial experts, and economists is as fatal to us as a decline in the output of textile operatives, fitters, and farmers. A poor and ineffective government would be as fatal to us as an incompetent master-mariner would be to the safety of one of our ships : the officers and the crew might perhaps ' carry ' him in fair weather, but in foul he would probably cost them their lives and livelihood.

In some countries it is perhaps possible to say that one group of the nation is, or ought to be, independent of others. No one ought to say that in Britain. Just as Britain is more dependent for her material standard of life on world trade than any other nation, so are her own people more *interdependent* than the peoples of other nations. They are a more highly industrialized, more internationally trading people even than the Americans, who still have a larger percentage of people earning a living from farms and primary-producing occupations. So the British, more even than the Americans, have the biggest material stake in raising the productivity of their industry.

That is a joint and several task, for in modern industry the parts are becoming more and more simplified, sub-divided, and specialized. The finished product is becoming more and more the result of assembly. For the British this means more— not less—interdependence. It means more—not less—co-operation, teamwork, and more of a flow in production. It means that in order to survive in the increasingly competitive world where they must trade—and in order to maintain (let alone to improve) their material standards of life—the British must continuously raise the fruitfulness, the efficiency of the work of machines and men : the work which they all do to turn out the exports, the equipment, the essential expert and other services, the education, the skills, and the goods themselves.

(approx. 500 words)

We Too Can Prosper : GRAHAM HUTTON

20

Give the substance of the following article in about 200 words.

TURBOJETS

When the Gas Turbine emerged about twelve years ago there was reason to suppose that its apparent simplicity would herald a profusion of different designs and so enable the new power form, with or without propellers, to be tailored to particular aircraft projects. Certainly in principle the engine is simple enough : a single shaft joins a compressor at the front to a turbine at the back. Between them is a continuously burning flame and the turbine collects energy from the heated and expanding gas to drive the compressor, leaving enough residual energy free to escape and propel the vehicle. But in the early days gas turbines often refused to work at all, and despite all encouragement they remained obstinately inert. Later, the gas was persuaded to provide enough power to turn the compressor, and gradually, after refinements, some positive thrust was produced. In due course, one pound of thrust could be generated for each pound of engine weight. The figure has steadily improved and now five pounds of thrust for every pound of engine weight can be achieved : indeed industry expects that later more than one pound of thrust will be obtained for every pound weight of the entire aircraft, so leading to fighters that can push themselves off the ground without forward run. Meanwhile improvements in fuel consumption have been made ; until recently one pound of thrust required one and a quarter pounds of kerosene fuel, but now only one pound of fuel is needed. Naturally the penalty for these advances lay in increasing the maze of complexity. The compressor, for instance, instead of being forged from a single solid is now composed of hundreds of precision-formed blades —originally in aluminium, now in steel and titanium. The compressor of the 10,000 lb. thrust Bristol Olympus embodies the further principle of duality—each half driven through concentric shafts at different speeds by separate turbines with only a gas connection between them.

Time has shown that the task of evolving a big gas turbine demands fifteen to twenty times the effort that went into the most complicated piston engines. A high proportion of these additional engineering and design man-hours has been spent in unremitting search towards a better understanding of how to handle enormous volumes of air. Instead of using fifteen parts of air to one of fuel as in a piston engine, the gas turbine uses eighty-five parts of air. And naturally the science of guiding air into the engine through the intake with minimum losses is as important as reducing duct losses and turbulence when it is inside the engine. Apart from the aerodynamics, the science of turbine metallurgy has also been in a state of constant change. Early in the career of the gas turbine, aluminium alloys had to be replaced by various chrome and cobalt steels and nickel alloys. Some of these have scarcely had an opportunity to prove themselves before they, in turn, have been overtaken by the properties of titanium, whose immensely important alloys are midway between aluminium and steel in weight and approaching steel in strength.

The result is that new types of turbine engines are now taking some five to seven years to develop, and the gap is widening between the capabilities of 7-10,000 lb. engines in production and those with three times the power which are now feasible. Discoveries follow each other in quick succession and there is no hint anywhere that this characteristic pace in turbine technology is slackening. The Engine Division of the Bristol Aeroplane Company is balancing the rapidly expanding frontiers of scientific knowledge with the cycle of production that follows long afterwards in its wake.

From an advertisement of the Bristol Aeroplane Co. Ltd.

21

Make a précis of the following correspondence.

Letter No. 1.

BRADFORD ROAD,
LEEDS, 2.
18th March, 1954.

MESSRS. WILLIAMSON & SONS,
    FISHERGATE,
        PRESTON,
            LANCS.

Dear Sirs,

Thank you for your letter of 16th March offering us a parcel of mahogany subject to prompt reply by return of post.

Unhappily, a reply by return could not be sent as the manager was away from business.

However, we should be glad to accept the offer providing that you can deliver in two lots—half immediately, and the balance at the end of next month.

If you agree, please telegraph us upon receipt of this letter, as we have had another parcel offered to us which we shall probably take up if we do not come to terms with you.

                Yours faithfully,
           FRANK BOWYER & COMPANY.

Telegram from Williamson & Sons to Frank Bowyer & Company :

            Bowyer — Leeds.
Agree to your terms—writing. WILLSONIAN.

Letter No. 2.

Telegraphic Address :   FISHERGATE,
'WILLSONIAN,' PRESTON.   PRESTON.
                          19*th March*, 1954.

MESSRS. FRANK BOWYER & COMPANY,
    BRADFORD ROAD,
        LEEDS, 2.

Dear Sirs,

Thank you for your letter of 18th March and, although our special offer was for prompt delivery, we decided to accept your conditions

E

A telegram (which we now confirm) to this effect was sent you this morning.

Awaiting your official order-sheet in due course,

We are, Dear Sirs,

Yours faithfully,

WILLIAMSON & SONS.

Letter No. 3.

BRADFORD ROAD,

LEEDS, 2.

20th March, 1954.

MESSRS. WILLIAMSON & SONS,

FISHERGATE,

PRESTON,

LANCS.

Dear Sirs,

Thank you for your telegram received this morning from which it is noted that you accept the conditions of delivery regarding the parcel of mahogany as set forth in our letter of the 18th March.

Official order-sheet No. S. 987 is enclosed.

Yours faithfully,

FRANK BOWYER & COMPANY.

Letter No. 4.

BRADFORD ROAD,

LEEDS, 2.

19th April, 1954.

MESSRS WILLIAMSON & SONS,

PRESTON.

Dear Sirs,

Order No. S. 987.

Cheque is enclosed for your invoice of 22nd March. Please acknowledge receipt.

Although the second half of the mahogany was not to be delivered until the end of the month, we shall be glad if you will

dispatch it now as a contract has been placed with us which
will enable us to use it immediately.

Yours faithfully,

FRANK BOWYER & COMPANY.

[W.R.C.C.]

22

State as briefly as possible in simple English exactly what
the following contract is about, taking particular care not to
miss any important feature :

MEMORANDUM OF AGREEMENT

made this fifth day of September One thousand nine hun-
dred and nineteen BETWEEN Patrick Mangan of Sukotra,
Chislehurst in the County of Kent (hereinafter called " the
Landlord ") of the one part and William Blake of Ander-
sham Hall in the County of Norfolk (hereinafter called
" The Tenant ") of the other part.   WHEREBY the
Landlord agrees to let and the Tenant agrees to take ALL
that flat situate and being 29, Northfield Avenue, Kensington,
in the County of London, together with the use of the
Entrance Hall and Staircase in common with the remaining
Tenants and the use and enjoyment of all the Furniture
Fixtures Utensils and things more particularly enumerated
and set forth in an Inventory to be signed by Tenant for the
purpose of identification TO HOLD the same for a term of
six calendar months from the seventh day of September One
thousand nine hundred and nineteen at the clear weekly
rental of four guineas ($£4/4/-$) payable every three calendar
months in advance the first of such payments amounting to
fifty four pounds twelve shillings to be made immediately on
the signing hereof And the Tenant also further agrees to pay
for all gas and electric light consumed on the premises during
his Tenancy including all stove and meter rents and that he
will not permit to be done on the premises anything which shall
be a breach of any of the covenants or conditions contained in
the Superior Agreement under which the premises are held by
the Landlord and particularly will not permit any waste or
damage to be done thereon or anything which may be or

become a nuisance or annoyance to the Landlord or his Superior Landlord or any of the adjoining Tenants, or permit the same to be used for any illegal purpose or for any purpose other than as a private residence And that he will not assign underlet or part with the possession of the premises or any part thereof. PROVIDED always and it is hereby agreed that in the event of the rents hereby reserved or any portion thereof being in arrear (whether legally demanded or not) or if there shall be any breach of the covenants and conditions on the part of the Tenant herein before contained or if the Tenant shall become subject to the Bankruptcy Laws then and in any of such cases it shall be lawful for the Landlord immediately thereupon to re-enter upon the premises, or any part thereof in the name of the whole and to expel the said Tenant and all other persons therefrom without bringing any action for ejectment or taking any other proceedings at Law for the recovery of such possession and that thenceforth this Agreement shall be utterly void but without prejudice to the right of action of the Landlord in respect of any antecedent breach of the Tenant's agreements herein contained. And the Tenant hereby further agrees to leave upon the said premises at the termination of the Tenancy hereby created the several Furniture Fixtures Utensils Plate Linen and things mentioned in the before referred to Inventory in as good state and condition as the same now are (reasonable wear and tear and damage by fire only excepted) and that he will replace such part of them as shall be broken or damaged with similar goods of equal value or allow a sufficient sum to cover the cost of such damage or breakage And that he will have cleaned all the washable articles in the flat or allow a sufficient sum to cover the cost of same. And that he will leave the said Furniture and articles mentioned in the said Inventory in the rooms in which they now are And that he will during a period of two weeks prior to the expiration of the Tenancy permit inspection of the flat at any reasonable hour of the day by any person desirous of becoming a Tenant thereof. Failing the receipt by the Landlord or his Agent of two clear weeks notice in writing prior to the expiration of the Tenancy granted the tenancy shall be deemed to continue from month to month upon similar terms and conditions to those hereinbefore stated determinable by two weeks notice in writing on either side such notice to expire only on the 7th day in any month the rent always to be paid monthly in advance And the Landlord further agrees with the Tenant that on the due performance by the Tenant of the above mentioned agreements and stipulations on his part he the Tenant shall have quiet enjoyment of the said premises during the said Tenancy free from interruption by the Landlord or any person legally claiming through or under him.

The LANDLORD agrees with the Tenant to pay the rent and perform and observe the agreements contained in the Superior Agreement under which the premises are held by the Landlord.

IN WITNESS whereof the said parties to these presents have hereunto set their hand the day and year first above written.

Signed by the within named

   PATRICK MANGAN

in the presence of

   JAMES STEVENSON

     Barrister at law

     Princes Risborough

       LONDON

Part Eight: COMPREHENSION

I

Read the following passage carefully two or three times, and then answer the questions on it :

I liked Mr. Parfitt for his merry, crinkled smile, for his craftsman's love of his trade (even though it was a dishonest trade), and because he never cheated anybody who did not deserve to be cheated.

5 He had a shop in the unfashionable part of the town. Over the door hung the simple, austere and untruthful sign, " ANTIQUES." You went into a small low room which was always very dark—it had to be dark—and out of the shadows came shuffling the small, wizened

10 form of Mr. Parfitt. He peered at you with bright, inquisitive eyes and asked rather tersely what you wanted. He was never obsequious to his customers ; indeed he always seemed reluctant to sell anything ; once he wept at parting with a fine old Welsh dresser

15 which, he said was his proudest possession. His tears were not faked, though the dresser was ; he had spent long days and nights fashioning it with skill and ingenuity and loving care from some odd bits of old, dark oak. He knew all the old tricks of the trade and

20 had some of his own. If in 1930 you bought from him one of those much admired convex mirrors, period 1800, and took the precaution of removing the glass, you would find behind it a piece of newspaper bearing a date somewhere near 1800, for he had amassed pieces

25 of newspaper of various dates for this very purpose.

It was Mr. Parfitt who discovered the El Dorado of the old town's tourist trade. Others copied him, but he, who blazed the trail, continued to reap a grand harvest from it, ever mining deeper into the tourists'

30   pockets and extracting new deposits of gold.

(a) In about forty of **your own words**, without detail or illustration, state what were Mr. Parfitt's more attractive and what his less attractive characteristics.

(b) Explain the meaning of **three** of the following as used in the passage : (i) wizened (line 9) ; (ii) tersely line 11) ; (iii) obsequious (line 12) ; (iv) fashioning (line 17) ; (v) tricks of the trade (line 19).

(c) Answer **three** of the following questions. (i) Why was it advisable for Mr. Parfitt's shop to be in the unfashionable part of the town ? (ii) Why had his room to be dark ? (iii) Why did it help him to seem reluctant to sell ? (iv) Why was he really reluctant to sell the Welsh dresser ?

(d) Explain Mr. Parfitt's trick with the mirror.

(e) In any metaphor there is a point of similarity between two otherwise dissimilar objects or ideas. Illustrate this statement by explaining the metaphors : (i) " the El Dorado of the old town's tourist trade " (lines 26-27) ; (ii) " blazed the trail " (line 28).

(f) State, with a reason, whether you think the metaphor " reap a grand harvest " is in keeping with the rest of the sentence or not.

                                                    J.M.B.

II

Read the following passage carefully and then answer the questions that follow.

        I say we have despised science. ' What ! ' you exclaim ' are we not foremost in all discovery, and is not the whole world giddy by reason, or unreason, of our inventions ? ' Yes ; but do you suppose that is
5   national work ? That work is all done in spite of the nation ; by private people's zeal and money. We are glad enough, indeed, to make our profit of science ; we snap up anything in the way of a scientific bone that has meat on it, eagerly enough ; but if the scientific man

10 comes for a bone or crust to us ; that is another story.
What have we publicly done for science ? We are
obliged to know what o'clock it is, for the safety of our
ships, and therefore we pay for an observatory ; and
we allow ourselves, in the person of our Parliament, to
15 be annually tormented into doing something, in a
slovenly way, for the British Museum ; sullenly apprehending that to be a place for keeping stuffed birds in,
to amuse our children. If anybody will pay for their
own telescope, and resolve another nebula, we cackle
20 over their discernment as if it were our own ; if one in
ten thousand of our hunting squires suddenly perceives
that the earth was indeed made to be something else
than a portion for foxes, and burrows in it himself, and
tells us where the gold is, and where the coals, we
25 understand that there is some use in that ; and very
properly knight him : but is the accident of his having
found out how to employ himself usefully any credit
to *us* ?

(a) In about 80 of your own words give the reasons why
Ruskin accused England of despising science.

(b) Write a paragraph expanding the idea " Is not the
whole world giddy by reason, or unreason, of our
inventions ? " You may apply this to either Ruskin's
day or to our own time.

(c) Give the meaning of these words or phrases as used in
the passage :
observatory (line 13) ; apprehending (line 16) ; resolve
another nebula (line 19) ; discernment (line 20).

(d) Take one sentence or phrase where you consider Ruskin
to be most sarcastic. Explain the sarcasm.

III

Read the following passage carefully, and then answer the
questions on it :
There are many schools of walking ; one is that of
the road-walkers, but to my thinking they have grasped

only a part of the truth. The road is invaluable for
pace and swing, and the ideal walk demands a smooth
5   surface for some considerable portion of the way. On
other terms it is hard to cover a respectable distance,
and a road—like other ways—provides a change of
tactile values underfoot which is agreeable.

I insist, however, that road-walking is but a small
10   part of the whole art : twenty-five miles of wood and
fieldpath are better in every way than thirty-five hammered out on the road. The secret beauties of nature
are unveiled only to the cross-country walker : the
sudden glory of a woodland glade, the slow stream
15   murmuring its sweet refrain, the roaring torrent, the
early-morning autumnal tears on the bracken—these
and a thousand other blessed chances of the day are
the very heart of walking, and these are not of the
road. Yet the hard road plays a part in every good
20   walk ; nor must we forget the " soft " road, the broad
grass-tracks, relics of medieval wayfaring.

It is well to seek as much variety as possible in a
day's walking. Road and track, field and wood, hill
and plain, should follow each other in shifting vision.
25   But variety is not all : I scarcely know whether most
to value the aloofness and magic in the country I have
never seen before, or the familiar joys of country where
every tree and rock are rooted in the memories that
make up my life.

(a) Summarise, without detail or illustration, in about fifty
   of **your own words** the writer's ideas of how to
   obtain the fullest enjoyment from walking.

(b) Give the meaning of **three** of the following words as
   used in the passage, and for each of the words you
   choose write a sentence in which it is used with a
   different meaning :
   (i) terms (line 6) ; (ii) ways (line 7) ; (iii) refrain
   (line 15) ; (iv) part (line 19).

(c) Explain the meaning of **two** of the following :

E*

      (i) blessed chances of the day (line 17) ; (ii) these are not of the road (lines 18, 19) ; (iii) relics of medieval wayfaring (line 21).

(d) Choose **three** of the following words and state what comparison underlies the metaphorical use of each of the three in the passage : grasped (line 2) ; (ii) hammered (line 11) ; (iii) unveiled (line 13) ; (iv) tears (line 16) ; (v) heart (line 18) ; (vi) rooted (line 28).

(e) In the essay from which it is taken the passage is preceded by the sentence " I have two doctors, my left leg and my right, and when body and mind are creaking, I know that I have only to summon my doctors and I shall be well again."

Write a version of this sentence without using any metaphors, and give one reason why you think it is, or is not, a good introduction to the passage.

                                     J.M.B.

IV

1.—Summarize, reducing it to about one third of the original the following passage (which contains about 460 words), using either direct or indirect speech, and assigning a **short** appropriate title.   You are advised to devote about 15 minutes to reading the passage, and about 30 minutes to writing the précis.   Count, carefully, the number of words you use, and write the number at the end of your précis.

      During the Tudor reigns England changed her national weapon.   She laid aside the long-bow and acquired the broadside.   The long-bow, that had rendered her soldiers superior to all others in Europe,
5   had lured her into a hundred years of military adventure in France.   The broadside—the rows of cannon protruding from the ship's timbers—showed her a better way, along the paths of the ocean to new lands.   By the broadside, sea warfare was completely

10   changed. The ship ceased to be a platform for a storm-
ing party and became a moving battery of guns.

      This change in the character of warfare at sea was
better understood and more quickly exploited by the
English than by their enemies. The Spaniards had
15   Mediterranean traditions connected with the oared
galley and the grappling of ship to ship. These ancient
and honourable traditions hampered Spanish seaman-
ship, even after Philip improvised an ocean-going navy
to conquer England in the Atlantic and the Channel.
20   His armada was, in its real spirit, an army embarked ;
the soldiers outnumbered and bullied the sailors, regarding them as mechanic drudges, whose privilege it
was to bring the gallant *soldado* to grips with his enemy.

      But in the English fleet—commanded by Howard,
25   Frobisher, Hawkins, Drake—the Admiral and his
Captains were seamen and they were in full command
of everyone on board. The soldiers were few and knew
their place at sea. Drake, on his voyage round the
world (1577-1580) had established the rule that even
30   the gentleman volunteer must haul at the ropes with
the mariner. The discipline and equality of the crew
at sea were accepted by the Englishman, while the
Spaniard could not lay aside his military and aristocratic
pride even to save the ship. It was a social difference
35   between the countries, translated into terms of war.

      The fighting merchant ship, accustomed to defend
herself and to force her trade in all the waters of the
world, took a large share in the battle against the
Armada, but without the Queen's own professional
40   warships the victory could not have been won. In
a fortunate hour (1578) Elizabeth put John Hawkins
in charge of the building and upkeep of her ships.
This great public servant well understood what kind
of ships he ought to build for the new kind of warfare.
45   His critics, clinging to the ideas of an older school,
clamoured for vessels with a high superstructure,
impregnable to assault but difficult to manoeuvre.

I had thought of the possibility of northerly winds bringing a swell, but had argued, first, that no heavy northerly swell had ever been recorded in the Sound ;
5   secondly, that a strong northerly wind was bound to bring pack which would damp the swell ; thirdly, that the locality was excellently protected by the Barne Glacier ; and finally, that the beach itself showed no signs of having been swept by the sea, the rock frag-
10   ments composing it being completely angular.

When the hut was erected and I found that its foundation was only 11 feet above the level of the sea ice, I had a slight misgiving, but reassured myself again by reconsidering the circumstances that afforded shelter
15   to the beach.

The fact that such a question had been considered made it easier to understand the attitude of mind that readmitted doubt in the face of phenomenal conditions.

The event has justified my original arguments, but
20   I must confess a sense of having assumed security without sufficient proof in a case where an error of judgment might have had dire consequences.

It was not until I found all safe at the Home Station that I realised how anxious I had been concerning it.
25   In a normal season no thought of it having been in danger would have occurred to me, but since the *loss* of the ponies and the breaking of the Glacier Tongue I could not rid myself of the fear that misfortune was in the air and that some abnormal swell had swept the
30   beach ; gloomy thoughts of the havoc that might have been wrought by such an event would arise in spite of the sound reasons which had originally led me to choose the site of the hut as a safe one.

Personal Journals : CAPTAIN R. F. SCOTT.

(1) In about 40 of **your own words** give the reasons why Scott thought the site of the hut was safe.

(2) Give the meaning of **Three** of these words as used in the passage :

swell (line 3) ; misgiving (line 13) ; security (line 20) ; dire (line 23).

(3) Give in your own words the meaning of the third paragraph, " The fact . . . conditions."

(4) What was (a) the event (line 19) ; and (b) such an event (line 31).

(5) Write not more than ten lines on the character of Captain Scott as judged from this passage.

VI

Read the following passage carefully, and then answer the questions on it :

When we are accused of forgetfulness, we might refute the accusation by enumerating all the things we have remembered during the day.

5   It is not from mere forgetfulness that we leave articles in public conveyances. From the list of articles so left we might assume that sportsmen have worse memories than their fellows, for it always includes a large number of footballs, cricket bats and fishing rods. When their owners are returning from
10   an afternoon's sport, their imaginations are absorbed with the vision of the day's doings, their heads among the stars or their hearts in their boots. Anglers are said—with what justification I do not know—to be the most imaginative of men, and the man who is
15   inventing magnificent lies is bound to be a little absent-minded. The fishing-rod of reality is forgotten as he day-dreams over the feats of the fishing-rod of Utopia.

Men with fallible memories like to think they are
20   by that very token superior to their fellows. A man, they say, who is a perfect remembering machine is seldom a man of first-rate intelligence. That's a " sour grapes " sort of argument, merely a cloak to conceal their poverty. I imagine that all the great thinkers

25   and writers and composers had exceptional powers of
      memory, though they may have refused to exercise
      them on the trivialities of the daily round.

(a) Express in **your own words** the substance of the second
    and third paragraphs (lines 4-18 and 19-27) of the
    above passage, dealing with them separately and
    using about 25 words for each.

(b) Express the meaning of **three** of the following words
    or expressions as used in this passage : (i) public
    conveyances (line 5) ; (ii) absorbed (line 10) ; (iii)
    justification (line 13) ; (iv) fallible (line 19).

(c) Choose **two** of the following, explain their meaning in
    the passage and show why that meaning is suggested
    by the metaphors or references they contain : (i) their
    heads . . . their boots (lines 11 and 12) ; (ii) The
    fishing-rod of reality . . . Utopia (lines 16 to 18) ;
    (iii) That's a " sour grapes " sort of argument (lines
    22 and 23).

(d) Explain how " enumerating all the things remembered
    during the day " refutes the accusation (lines 2 and 3).

(e) Suggest one instance of what the writer may have had
    in mind when he speaks of " the trivialities of the
    daily round " (line 27).

                                                J.M.B.

VII

Read the following passage carefully and then answer the
questions which follow.

      The public is entitled to know of the vast strides
which have been made by scientific advances in criminal
detection, of the training that is given to the detective
officer in modern schools like that at the Metropolitan
5   Police College, at Eynsham in Oxford, at Wakefield and
elsewhere.   The officer who comes out of these schools
is trained to spot the slightest deviation from the normal
—a thread of cloth caught on a window-sill, a solitary
hair on a curtain, a finger print, a pinhead of blood or

10   the smear of lipstick or saliva, a flake of paint or the
      merest trace of a metal dust ground off a safe-breaker's
      tool—any of these, or more probably several of them
      together, may undo the perfect crime. In these days
      the criminal's chances of making a steady living are
15   thin and the super-crook has virtually disappeared.
      Crime has been on the increase—but so also have arrests
      and convictions, a fact often left out of the reproaches
      levelled at the police forces. Crime will always exist,
      but the real measure of any success the police may
20   achieve must be their ability to cramp the free style of
      the habitual criminal. He may be cunning and may
      expend much care and thought in planning his coup, but
      he is matching his brain and slender resources against
      all the might of a vast police network with infinite
25   resource, and an efficiency the envy of the world.
          It would be sensational to say that a murderer was
      " hanged by a thread ", an " ear of barley in the turnup
      of a trouser " or a trivial slip that left some vital clue at
      the scene of the crime, but it is rare for this to be so ;
30   indeed the Director of Public Prosecutions would be
      likely to " offer no evidence " for a prosecution if it was
      so slender—it would not be enough to convince a jury of
      guilt. What does convict is a series of trivialities and the
      backing of circumstantial evidence that accumulates
35   from the taking of statements—often by the score or
      hundred. Few people who absorb the headline " hanged
      by a hair " realise the patience in collecting and sifting
      evidence that goes on steadily from the moment a body
      is found to the hoped-for sequel when a suspect is
40   charged.

                                        (approx. 390 words)

  (a) Summarise the above passage in about a quarter of its
      length. State in brackets at the end the number of
      words you have used.

  (b) What are " the reproaches levelled at the police forces "
      (lines 17, 18) ?

(c) Write two paragraphs, each about eight lines in length
    to illustrate these phrases : police network (line 24) ;
    sifting evidence (lines 37, 38).

(d) Give the meaning of these words or phrases as they are
    used in the passage :
    virtually (line 15) ; series of trivialities (line 33) ;
    circumstantial evidence (line 34) ; accumulates (line
    34) ; sequel (line 39).

VIII

Read the following passage carefully and then answer the
questions which follow :

This has been called the age of electricity, for
electricity is now used for such a variety of purposes
that it appears to be able to replace all other agencies
for doing things. It has caused many changes both
5   inside and outside our homes, but the developments in
science which a fuller knowledge of electricity has
brought about are even more extensive and fundamental,
though they are not so much in the public eye.

Let us consider briefly some of the most obvious and
10   general changes which are due to the use of electricity.
The last century was boastfully spoken of as the Age
of Steam, for steam power had grown from small
beginnings until it transformed the whole course of
manufacture and trade, and had caused the Industrial
15   Revolution. For the first time, power to drive machines
was made available at a low cost. This power, however,
had to be used close to the spot where it was generated.
The tendency was to make factories larger and larger
for the sake of economy, and the workpeople were
20   compelled to live near these factories, for there was no
quick transport. Also, in the days of steam, the power
in the factories had to be distributed to the machines
by shafts and belts, which were cumbersome and
dangerous and, owing to friction, wasteful of power.

25   Nowadays the transmission of power by electricity has
      brought about a great change. This change is due to two
      facts : first, power can be transmitted to a great
      distance with practically negligible loss if it is carried by
      an electric current ; secondly, power can be converted
30   from mechanical form to the electrical form and back
      again to the mechanical form with almost 100 per cent
      efficiency. These two facts explain the preference for
      electricity in industry today.

                                              (300 words)

(a) Summarise the above passage in about a quarter of its
     length. State in brackets at the end the number of
     words you have used.
(b) " the developments in science which a fuller knowledge
     of electricity has brought about are even more
     extensive and fundamental ". Add to this statement
     about ten lines in which you give three examples not
     mentioned in the passage.
(c) Explain what the writer means in lines 27 to 32,
     " power . . . efficiency."
(d) Give the meaning of **Five** of the following words as
     they are used in the passage :
     fundamental (line 7) ; generated (line 17) ; economy
     (line 19) ; cumbersome (line 23) ; friction (line 24) ;
     transmission (line 25) ; negligible (line 28).

                              IX

Read the following passage carefully, and then answer the
questions on it.
      The regret we have for our childhood is not wholly
      justifiable : so much a man may lay down without
      fear of public ridicule ; for although we may shake
      our heads over the change, we are not unconscious
5   of the manifold advantages of our new state. The
      capacity to enjoy Shakespeare may balance a lost

aptitude for playing at soldiers. Terror is gone out of our lives, moreover ; we no longer see the devil in the bed-curtains, nor lie awake to listen to the
10 wind. We go to school no more ; and if we have only exchanged one drudgery for another (which is by no means sure), we are set free for ever from the daily dread of chastisement. And yet a great change has overtaken us ; and although we do not enjoy our-
15 selves less, at least we take our pleasures differently. We need pickles nowadays to make Monday's cold mutton please our Wednesday's appetite ; and I can remember the time when to call it red venison, and tell myself a hunter's story, would have made it more
20 palatable than the best of sauces. To the grown person, cold mutton is cold mutton all the world over ; not all the myths invented by man will make it better or worse for him ; the broad fact, the insistent reality, of the mutton carries away before it such
25 seductive figments. But for the child it is still possible to weave an enchantment over eatables ; and if he has but read of a dish in a story-book, it will be heavenly manna to him for a week.

(a) State in general terms, without detailed illustration, in about forty of your own words, what the writer thinks we gain and what we lose in becoming adults.

(b) Show by definition the exact meaning in the passage of **three** of the following : (i) manifold (line 5) ; (ii) aptitude (line 7) ; (iii) palatable (line 20) ; (iv) seductive (line 25) ; (v) figments (line 25).

(c) Why should the writer speak particularly of a Wednesday's appetite (line 17) ?

(d) What idea is conveyed by the expression " shake our heads over " (lines 3, 4) ?

(e) For **three** of the following give other expressions to convey the same idea : (i) public ridicule (line 3) ; (ii) dread of chastisement (line 13) ; (iii) myths (line 22) ; (iv) heavenly manna (lines 27, 28).

(f) The writer implies that a child's mind and an adult's
mind tend to have different outlooks : bring out
this difference by expressing each outlook in a word
or short phrase.

(g) Choose which of the following titles seems to you most
suitable for the passage, and for each of the other two
give a reason why you think it less suitable :

    (i) The pleasures of eating.

    (ii) From childhood to manhood.

    (iii) Make-believe.   J.M.B.

X

Read the following passage carefully and then answer the
questions that follow.

In our day, man's technology is keeping its maker on
the run. Our technological feat of " annihilating distance " is having the same effect as a rapidly rising
flood. The world's population is being crowded together
5 on the patch of ground that still stands above flood-level.
But as the waters rise, the patch shrinks and the refugees
are compressed into ever closer quarters. When this
happens in non-human life, the animals who have found
a common refuge on the island are said to observe,
10 instinctively, a temporary " truce of God." The lion
really does lie down with the lamb till the flood-waters
subside. In our present human quandary, however, a
merely temporary truce is not going to save us from
bringing on ourselves the fate of the Kilkenny cats ; for
15 the progress of technology shows no signs of abating.
So, human-fashion, we must supplement instinct by art.
Now that we are all going to be within point-blank
H-bomb range of one another permanently, we have to
train ourselves to live together like one of those " happy
20 families " in a menagerie, where the hunter and the
hunted—lion and lamb, cat and mouse, hawk and dove
—do live permanently cheek-by-jowl within one narrow
common cage, not thanks to an instinct that comes into

play only in emergencies, but thanks to patient training,
25 from infancy, by skilful human educators.

Here is the model of the small and crowded world in
which mankind is going to find itself in the chapter of
history that is opening in our time ; and this new
situation calls for new views and new policies. It calls,
30 for instance, for a drastic revision of the current Western
view of what is the standard and normal pattern of
mankind's geographical distribution. In the West we
see the world as a patch-work quilt made up of national
units, each of them displaying a distinctive colour of
its own, and each of them separated by a sharp dividing
40 line from the different-coloured patches adjoining it.
This has never, of course, been the prevailing pattern of
distribution in the world at large ; it has been prevalent
just in Western Europe ; and, in the aeroplane age, it
is rapidly being transformed, even here, into the quite
45 different pattern of a piece of shot silk, in which threads
of different colours are interwoven. In Western Europe,
as elsewhere, the multinational state, not the national
state, is going to be the normal standard pattern of the
future ; and the hunter and the hunted—Gentile and
50 Jew, Protestant and Catholic, Christian and Muslim,
White and Black—are going to be intermingled there.
They are going to be parked, cheek-by-jowl, in the same
streets and the same tenement houses, and they are
going to have to learn to live at very close quarters
55 without scratching one another's eyes out.

(approx. 470 words)

(a) Summarise the above passage in about a quarter of its
length. State in brackets at the end the number of
words you have used.

(b) Show that you understand the second sentence in the
passage by explaining " our technological feat of
' annihilating distance ' ", and show what is its effect
according to the author of the passage.

(c) (i) What is meant by a " truce of God " (line 10) ?

(ii) What do you think was " the fate of the Kilkenny cats " (line 14) ?

(iii) What is the reason given for the " happy families " in a menagerie " (line 20) ?

(d) Give briefly the meaning of **Four** of the following words or phrases as they are used in the passage :

technology (line 1) ; quandary (line 12) ; supplement (line 16) ; cheek-by-jowl (line 22) ; prevalent (line 42) ; the multinational state (line 47).

XI

Night is a dead monotonous period under a roof ; but in the open world it passes lightly, with its stars and dews and perfumes, and the hours are marked by changes in the face of Nature. What seems
5　a kind of temporal death to people choked between walls and curtains, is only a light and living slumber to the man who sleeps afield. All night long he can hear Nature breathing deeply and freely ; even as she takes her rest, she turns and smiles ; and there is one
10　stirring hour unknown to those who dwell in houses when a wakeful influence goes abroad over the sleeping hemisphere, and all the outdoor world are on their feet. It is then that the cock first crows, not this time to announce the dawn, but like a cheerful watchman
15　speeding the course of night. Cattle awake on the meadows ; sheep break their fast on the dewy hillsides, and change to a new lair among the ferns ; and houseless men who have lain down with the fowls, open their dim eyes and behold the beauty of the night.
20　At what inaudible summons, at what gentle touch of Nature, are all these sleepers thus recalled in the same hour to life ? Do the stars rain down an influence, or do we share some thrill of mother earth below our resting bodies ? Even shepherds or old country-folk,
25　who are the deepest read in the hidden secrets, have not a guess as to the purpose of this nightly resurrection.

Towards two in the morning they declare the thing takes place ; and neither know nor inquire further. And at least it is a pleasant incident. We are disturbed
30 in our slumber only, like the luxurious Montaigne " that we may the better and more sensibly relish it." We have a moment to look upon the stars. And there is a special pleasure for some minds in the reflection that we share the impulse with all outdoor creatures
35 in our neighbourhood, that we have escaped out of the Bastille of civilisation, and are become, for the time being, a mere kindly animal and a sheep of Nature's flock.

   Travels with a Donkey in the Cevennes : R. L. STEVENSON

(a) In forty of your own words tell why the author prefers sleeping outdoors.

(b) What is the " nightly resurrection " (line 27) ? In your own words give two causes the author suggests for it.

(c) What is the force of the adjective in the following :
   (i) temporal death (line 5) ; (ii) dim eyes (line 19) ; (iii) living slumber (line 6), inaudible summons (line 20) ?

(d) What is a hemisphere (line 12), and why is it a better word here than " world " ?

(e) Mention six ways in which the personification of Nature is shown in the passage.

(f) What picture is drawn in the simile " like a cheerful watchman speeding the course of night " (line 15) ?

(g) How far do you consider the following apt metaphors :
   (i) the Bastille of civilisation (line 36) ; (ii) a sheep of Nature's flock (lines 37, 38) ?

XII

The following verses are from Thomas Gray's " Elegy in a Country Churchyard." Read them carefully, and answer the questions printed below them.

The curfew tolls the knell of parting day,
The lowing herd wind slowly o'er the lea,
The ploughman homeward plods his weary way,
4   And leaves the world to darkness and to me.

Now fades the glimmering landscape on the sight,
And all the air a solemn stillness holds,
Save where the beetle wheels his droning flight,
8   And drowsy tinklings lull the distant folds ;

Save that from yonder ivy-mantled tower
The moping owl does to the moon complain
Of such as, wand'ring near her secret bower,
12   Molest her ancient solitary reign.

Beneath those rugged elms, that yew-tree's shade,
Where heaves the turf in many a mould'ring heap,
Each in his narrow cell for ever laid,
16   The rude Forefathers of the hamlet sleep.

The breezy call of incense-breathing Morn,
The swallow twitt'ring from the straw-built shed,
The cock's shrill clarion, or the echoing horn,
20   No more shall rouse them from their lowly bed.

For them no more the blazing hearth shall burn,
Or busy housewife ply her evening care ;
No children run to lisp their sire's return,
24   Or climb his knees the envied kiss to share.

Oft did the harvest to their sickle yield,
Their furrow oft the stubborn glebe has broke ;
How jocund did they drive their team afield
28   How bowed the woods beneath their sturdy stroke !

Let not Ambition mock their useful toil,
Their homely joys, and destiny obscure ;
Nor Grandeur hear, with a disdainful smile,
32   The short and simple annals of the poor.

The boast of heraldry, the pomp of power,
And all that beauty, all that wealth e'er gave,
Awaits alike th' inevitable hour.
36   The paths of glory lead but to the grave.

(a) Select **three** words or phrases which show that the poet is in a churchyard.

(b) What three words or phrases does the poet use to create an atmosphere of quietness?

(c) (i) What does the poet mean by the word " rude " in line 16? (ii) What is a " hamlet "? (iii) Explain " curfew."

(d) Why is the morning described as " incense-breathing " in line 17, and what is " the echoing horn " in line 19?

(e) What do you understand by " the short and simple annals of the poor " in line 32?

(f) Say what you understand by " ivy-mantled " (line 9) ; " shrill clarion " (line 19) ; " stubborn glebe " (line 26) ; " jocund " (line 27).

(g) Give one example of (i) metaphor (ii) personification (iii) alliteration.

(h) Paraphrase the last stanza.

[OXFORD AND CAMBRIDGE]

XIII

1.—Summarise, reducing it to about one-third of the original, the following passage (which contains about 450 words) using either direct or indirect speech, and assigning a short appropriate title.

Let us look at the true cottages of Wiltshire. There are, I imagine, few places in England where the humble homes of the people have so great a charm. Undoubtedly they are darker inside, and not so
5   convenient to live in as the modern box-shaped, red-brick, slate-roofed cottages which have spread a wave of ugliness over the country ; but they do not

offend—they please the eye. They are smaller than
the modern-built habitations ; they are weathered
10 and coloured by sun and wind and rain and many
lowly vegetable forms to a harmony with nature.
They appear related to the trees amid which they
stand, to the river and meadows, to the sloping downs
at the side, and to the sky and clouds over all.
15 And, most delightful feature, they stand among, and
are wrapped up in, flowers as in a garment—rose
and vine and creeper and clematis. They are mostly
thatched, but some have tiled roofs, their deep dark
red clouded and stained with lichen and moss ; and
20 these roofs, too, have their flowers in summer.

But the garden flowers are to me the best of all
flowers. The big house garden, or gardener's garden,
with everything growing in it I hate, but these I
love—fragrant gilly-flower and pink and clove-
25 smelling carnation ; wall-flower, abundant periwinkle,
sweet-william, larkspur, love-in-a-mist . . . and pansy.
And best of all and in greatest profusion that flower of
flowers, the marigold.

How the townsman, town born and bred, regards
30 this flower, I do not know. He is, in spite of all the
time I have spent in his company, a comparative
stranger to me—the one living creature on earth
who does not greatly interest me. Some over-populated
planet in our system discovered a way to relieve itself
35 by discharging its superfluous millions on our globe—
a pale people with hurrying feet and eager, restless
minds, who live apart in monstrous, crowded camps,
like wood ants that go not out to forage for themselves
—six millions of them crowded together in one camp
40 alone ! I have lived in these colonies, years and years,
never losing the sense of captivity, of exile, ever conscious of my burden, taking no interest in the doings
of that innumerable multitude. . . . What then, does it
matter how they regard this common orange-coloured
45 flower with a strong smell ? For me it has an atmosphere,

a sense or suggestion of something immeasurably remote and very beautiful.

But when my sight wanders away from the flower to others blooming with it—some so tall that they
50   reach quite up to the eaves of the lowly houses which they stand against—I begin to perceive that they all possess something of that magical quality.

W. H. Hudson

2.—The following questions are based on the above passage. Answer them briefly and, as far as possible, in complete statements in your own words :

  (a) Why does the writer prefer " the true cottages " (line 1) to those of the more modern type ?

  (b) Why do you think that he hated the " big house garden, or gardener's garden " ? (line 22).

  (c) What in your opinion, are the writer's chief objections to life in the town ?

  (d) What do you understand by the writer's personal reference : " ever conscious of my burden " ? (lines 41, 42).

  (e) What clues are there to the approximate date when the passage was written ?

3.—Explain carefully the meaning, in their contexts, of six of the following words and phrases from the passage, in complete sentences : weathered (line 9) ; a harmony with nature (line 11) ; lichen (line 19) ; a comparative stranger (lines 31, 32) ; some over-populated planet in our system (lines 33, 34) ; to forage for themselves (line 38) ; eaves (line 50) ; magical quality (line 52).

4.—From the passage in Question 1 answer these questions :

  (a) Comment on the writer's use of metaphor and simile. Select what you consider to be the most outstanding example of each, stating your reasons for your choice.

  (b) What devices of style does the writer use to add point

to his comments on the townsman ? Write a brief
note on these devices.

LONDON

XIV

Read the following poem carefully, and then answer the
questions on it.

> Say not the struggle naught availeth,
> The labour and the wounds are vain,
> The enemy faints not, nor faileth,
> And as things have been they remain.
>
> 5   If hopes were dupes, fears may be liars ;
> It may be, in smoke concealed,
> Your comrades chase e'en now the fliers,
> And, but for you, possess the field.
>
> For while the tired waves, vainly breaking,
> 10   Seem here no painful inch to gain,
> Far back, through creeks and inlets making,
> Comes silent, flooding in, the main :
>
> And not by eastern windows only,
> When daylight comes, comes in the light ;
> 15   In front, the sun climbs slow, how slowly,
> But westward, look, the land is bright !

(a) Express simply the thought contained in line 5 in about
twenty of **your own words**.

(b) Give equivalent expression for each of the following :

(i) the struggle naught availeth (line 1).

(ii) no painful inch to gain (line 10).

(c) Give a single word with the same meaning as *main* in
line 12.

(d) What does the metaphor of a moving tide suggest that
is so appropriate to the general thought of the poem ?

(e) Give in simple non-figurative language what the poet
wishes to suggest by the picture in lines 13-16.

(f) Explain the meaning of *flooding* as used in line 12.

(g) Select the phrase in the poem that emphasises the responsibility of the individual in achieving victory.

J.M.B.

XV

1.—Summarize, reducing it to about one-third of the original, the following passage (which contains about 500 words) using either direct or indirect speech, and assigning a short appropriate title.

To all of us nowadays it seems natural for boys and girls to go to school, and to learn writing and reading ; and in all educated homes they grow up surrounded by hundreds of books. It was not always so in England ;
5 compulsory education and girls' schools are very modern indeed.   Printed books are not yet five hundred years old. In early Greece, if there were any schools at all, they were only here and there ; and few indeed were those who went to them. It is a question
10 how many people could write, if any could. But it must not be supposed that people who cannot read or write are always uneducated or stupid ; very far from it. A man may load his memory with all kinds of things, and still be, as the English poet wrote,

15   The bookful blockhead, ignorantly read,
       With loads of learned lumber in his head.

If one looks at the things one has learnt, if one counts them, and then weighs them, it is surprising how much we learn out of school.   Simonides, one
20 of the older Greek poets, said : " The city teaches the man."   Without schools or books or playrooms, without examinations or newspapers, boys and sometimes girls learnt many things that modern boys and girls, yes, and modern men and women,
25 never learn.   Some things, no doubt, they learnt in the streets that did them no good.   But all round

them was real life. Men made things in the shop
fronts, and a boy could watch them. Here, in one
street, were the people who made sailcloth for the
30   ships ; and at the foot of it were shipyards, where
shipwrights and carpenters were building the ships of
wood ; and there is immense interest and education
in watching a boat being built. Then a sailor would
come along and talk to the boat-builder, and the
35   boy listened and heard wonderful tales of the sea and
the lands beyond it. Little as he thought it, the boy
was learning Geography, but he was also learning
something better. He was being taught to wonder ; and
wonder, said the Greeks, is the mother of thought.
40   There were no newspapers to tell what had not
happened ; but there were plenty of people to talk
as wildly about politics, to argue about nobility and
blood, about the price of food, about the need to change
the laws, about the bad ways of rulers and shop-keepers
45   and food-sellers and the need to fix the prices of everything, to let the poor live. And the boy could listen to
all of it, and note that, whatever argument one man
might use, another man could always argue for something different. Children grow up more intelligent to
50   this day in houses where things are argued out ; and
in every Greek street and market people argued, and
often talked sense, and the boy grew up with an instinct
for argument, and a quickness to see reason and to
trounce nonsense. The Greeks were born talkers, born
55   arguers, and loved to hear any new thing.

The Ancient World : T. R. GLOVER

2.—The following questions are based on the passage.
Answer them briefly and, as far as possible, in
complete statements in your own words :

(a) Explain carefully the meaning of the sentence " Wonder
is the mother of thought " (line 39), and give a
notable example of the truth of it.

(b) According to this passage, what **two** qualities of mind did a Greek develop in his youth ?

(c) What is the writer's opinion of the modern newspaper ? Give your reasons for agreeing or disagreeing with his opinion.

(d) Give your own views on the statement that " the city teaches the man " (lines 20, 21), stating whether you think it is true in modern times.

3.—

(a) Explain carefully the meaning, in their contexts, of **four** of the following words and phrases from the passage :

an instinct for argument (lines 52, 53) ; to trounce nonsense (line 54) ; ignorantly read (line 15) ; learned lumber (line 16) ; real life (line 27).

(b) Explain the following metaphors from the passage : load (line 13) ; weighs (line 18).

(c) Comment on the style of the verse quotation in lines 15-16.

LONDON